A HAWK IN THE SUN

Adventures Studying Hawks

Leon R. Powers

DIMI PRESS   Salem, Oregon

DIMI PRESS
3820 Oak Hollow Lane, SE
Salem, Oregon 97302-4774
503-364-7698
1-800-644-3464(orders only)

First Edition

Library of Congress Cataloging-in-Publication
Data

Powers, Leon R. (Leon Ray)
    A hawk in the sun : adventures studying
        hawks / Leon R. Powers.--1st ed.
        p. cm.
    ISBN 0-931625-40-8
        1. Ferruginous hawk. I. Title.

QL696.F32P72 2003
598.9'44--dc21

                                        2003046197

Cover design by Bruce DeRoos & Kara Thompson

Illustrations by Erica Craig

Printed in the United States of America
        10 9 8 7 6 5 4 3 2

"My question, answer in the fewest of words,

What sort of life is it among the birds?"

Aristophanes

"It is ironic that North America's largest and most powerful hawk is highly sensitive to human disturbance. Because of its unique niche, the ferruginous hawk is an excellent environmental barometer, with which scientists can forecast the future of sagebrush and grassland habitats in western North America. Living off the bounty of a fragile, rapidly changing ecosystem, the ferruginous hawk hangs on in tough times when prey is scarce and proliferates under good conditions. It is a survivor.

"Dr. Leon Powers creates a template for how a careful scientist gathers information without impacting the animal that fascinated him in the first place. His deep respect for the natural world is reflected in his descriptions of the vistas and creatures that he encounters in southern Idaho and northern Utah. Through diligent investigation, Dr. Powers unlocks the mysteries of desert survival for the ferruginous hawk, with its remarkable physical adaptations to the searing desert sun. Throughout the book, there is reverence for a creature with an indomitable spirit. In a smooth and engaging way, Dr. Powers weaves a fabric of hawk, prey, landscape and human interaction that at once educates and captivates the reader. As his students already know, he makes learning fun. Read this story and you too will understand why "

Bruce Haak. Author
PIRATE OF THE PLAINS

CONTENTS

Preface vii

Acknowledgements ix

Prologue xi

1   A Desert Duel 1

2   The Ferrug—inous—what? 5

3   The Search is On 9

4   Camera Shy 17

5   Penelope, the Stay-at-Home Mom 25

6   Stumbling Onto a Ground Nest 33

7   Disaster Strikes Thrice 41

8   Eternal Enemies 47

9   Winged Marauders of the Night 53

10   Moving in Close 65

11   Good Housekeeping—Ferruginous
     Hawk Style 73

12   Surviving a Heat Wave 81

13   Beating the Heat—Adaptations to a
Hot Environment 105

14   On Wings Like Eagles 113

15   From a Far Valley 123

16   Side Shows and Serendipity 135

17   The Hawk, the Swoop, and the Hare
are One 155

Epilogue 173

Index 183

PREFACE

On the desk in front of me beside my computer lies a 312 page doctoral dissertation entitled *Nesting Behavior of the Ferruginous Hawk.* A long time ago I wrote that document from a heap of weathered, laboriously gathered field notes, sifting every word through the excruciating exactitude of scientific scrutiny. By its very nature it was hewn from raw data, filtered through cold intellect and penned into hard facts. In essence, it was written from the head. Even though it continues to gather dust in the very few locations its copies now reside, I suppose it served its pedagogical purpose, for it helped to earn me a Ph.D. in zoology, and paved the way to my long professorship at Northwest Nazarene University.

This book that you now hold in your hands is a complete metamorphosis of that earlier dissertation. This writing comes from the warmth of the heart, and shares with you the deeply personal labor of love that was long disguised as research. My daily adventures with Ferruginous Hawks changed my life as a naturalist and this book relates those adventures and reveals the story behind the dissertation. This is about my sojourn with the hawks, a story that is known only to the dusty hills of the valleys: Curlew, Blackpine, and Raft River. I hope that you will read this book and let the hawks touch your life as they did mine.

ACKNOWLEDGEMENTS

Bringing this book from a dream to reality has been a family effort. My wife Willa not only bore the brunt of my long absences from home and family during the research stage of this story, lending support at every turn, but also edited and consulted on much of the writing. My son Shane, and daughter Kara pooled their considerable photographic, artistic, and creative expertise to help refine some of the graphics of this book, particularly the cover. Ryan, my younger son, in his own quiet way buoyed my resolve to see this book to completion by his own enthusiastic entry into professional novel writing. I thank each of these family members for their loving support throughout this project.

I remain ever grateful to Tim Craig and Rich Howard for their enthusiastic help and willing participation in our many shared experiences within this story. I thank Tim also for his insightful suggestions and editorial comments on an earlier draft of this book. Diane Ronayne's encouragement and meticulous editorial skills sharpened the quality of this writing. I appreciate the thoughtful and helpful comments provided by Mark Hilliard, David H. Ellis and Laurene Standford on portions of earlier drafts of this book.

I am deeply grateful to Dr. Chuck Trost of Idaho State University who willingly accepted me, as a marginally qualified graduate student and then encouraged and mentored me through the Ph.D. educational experience surrounding this story. I hope this book in some measure validates the confidence he displayed in me and offers some reward for the risk he took in my behalf.

Warm thanks to Erica H. Craig for her creative and artistic portrayal of the subjects, spirit and adventures of parts of this story.

I am grateful to Dick Lutz, President of DIMI PRESS for his confidence that this is a story worth telling, and for shepherding this book through the publication process in a timely manner.

PROLOGUE

Last entry in my field notes – a farewell

10 July 1974   Penelope's nest—Wildcat Hills

(06:30)   Cool, windy morning. Arrive at the blind: no birds seen or heard in the immediate area. I am suddenly saddened by the realization that the nesting season and my association with Penelope are essentially over, forever. I guess the finality of this visit is beginning to sink in. I sit and watch—and listen.

(08:00)   Still nothing seen or heard of Penelope or her family here in her territory. Cast against the still vivid and recent memories of high desert drama and discovery here at this nest site, the sudden stillness and emptiness of this scene seem strangely forlorn. I leave the blind and stroll among the junipers and pungent shrubbery, drinking in the panorama as though these are my last minutes on earth. I doubt that I'll ever return to this spot.

Angling toward Penelope's old nest of last year, the heaviness I feel is granted a brief reprieve as I spy a young ferruginous hawk perched on the ground in the shade. About that time Penelope appears from the south, calling and circling overhead before landing on a nearby juniper. I approach and photograph her. I muse at the improbability that she ever recognized me as anything but a threatening intrusion. I guess that is the difference between us two animals. I marvel at her beauty and the wonder of her very existence and survival while, at best, she protests and decries my mere presence, regarding it as a threat to that existence.

Seeking an opportunity to take some pictures of her flying, I approach very close and flush her—not much luck with the photography but I mainly want to say farewell to Penelope. Each time I get too near she flies to another perch ten or fifteen meters away, calling all the while. That a wild ferruginous hawk remains so close is actually quite amazing—but this hawk is Penelope. To this magnificent bird etched against the blue of the desert sky, to this quintessential hawk in the sun, I bid farewell. I promise never to invade her privacy again.

(08:30)   As I solemnly walk out of the nesting territory, I see a huge rattlesnake sunning at the base of a clump of rabbit brush. It slithers beneath the shrub before I can ready the camera. I bid it farewell too—and mentally thank it for not taking up residency in my blinds (so many times I probed the darkness while entering the blinds in the predawn hour)!

Farewell Wildcat Hills—I have a story to tell.

This book is that story. If you are one whose heart can still be stirred by the presence of wild things or by the sight of remote, wild landscapes, then perhaps I have written this story for you.

MAP LEGEND

A - Nest where Chapter 1 - "Desert Duel" took place

B - "Camera Shy" nest (Chapter 4)

C - Old Barn Nest where "moonlight vigil" and "wild dogs" occurred

D - "Greasy Ground Nest"

E - Penelope's nest where close-up observations were recorded

F - Nest near Penelope's territory, where time-lapse photography and observations from a blind occurred

G & H - Two adjacent nests that provided important observations

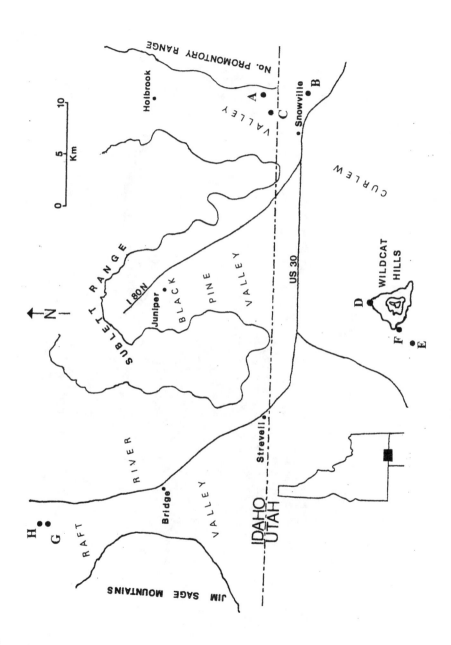

1

A Desert Duel

Aclash between the two desert predators seemed imminent. Immediately, my mind kicked into full alert at the very thought. For should a showdown unfold right here before me, I would be one of the privileged few ever to witness a contest between these two carnivores.

Partly concealed in the sage stood the regal, white-colored desert hawk, a stay-at-home mom. She was a ferruginous hawk, North America's largest buteo or broad-winged hawk, nearly two feet tall, weighing just under five pounds and with a wing span between four and five feet. This sleek female bird of prey was dauntless in defense of her young. I knew she pretty much ruled the skies around her territory. But would she rule the land as well?

Approaching from seventy-five yards out to the northeast, a much larger predator, a coyote, made its way into the heart of the hawk's nesting territory. I waited; I watched. I could feel myself tensing and my heart beginning to race—this was becoming an explosive setting! Silent and motionless, the alert hawk stood facing the intruder, watching it advance. As seconds ticked on, the distance separating the two melted away. Yet the hawk made no move to intercept the coyote.

The evening had begun like so many others I had spent watching this large desert hawk. I was concealed in a blind near her nest built atop a bushy, squat eight-foot juniper tree. The huge stick structure contained four well-feathered young. The nest tree was located at the east edge of Curlew Valley in southeastern Idaho, and the surrounding landscape was dotted by scattered sagebrush and crested wheat-grass.

For nearly two hours I had observed this territory from a distance, recording the activities of the young hawks in the nest. I also had noted the adult female hawk standing sentinel out on the ground, in a small clearing to the south. Nearly 100 yards from her nest tree, she had hardly moved, and only within the past couple of minutes had she pivoted to face the foothills to the northeast. As yet, her mate had not made an appearance at the nest and was presumably still hunting somewhere off in the distance, out of sight.

I had watched the female hawk for several minutes, peering through my forty-five power spotting scope. Then a rippling background movement caught my eye. Nearly 100 yards farther to the northeast, a coyote had come into view, ambling slowly toward the hawk and her nest. From my position, it looked as if the path of the coyote might take it directly to the nest tree. Perhaps it had caught the scent of prey remains in the nest or the young hawks themselves.

By now the coyote had worked its way past the hawk and seemed unaware of her presence. I was surprised at the deadly calm. "How about that," I thought. "She's going to let him pass unchallenged!"

Suddenly, seemingly out of nowhere, a flash of white wings exploded over the coyote's back, surprising it mid-stride. Dropping low to the ground and springing aside, the coyote spun to face the now-departing hawk. The male's whereabouts were no longer a mystery: I now knew where he was—and so did the intruding coyote!

Intent upon the male hawk's strafing, the coyote was caught completely off guard by the female, who now joined the fray by winging powerfully into a dive and dealing the coyote a stunning blow that raised a puff of dust from its back. Side-peddling to remain upright, the coyote immediately was strafed again by the plummeting male. Dodging, spinning, and snapping up at its winged assailants, the coyote was struck once again by the female hawk and nearly sent rolling across the grass.

Glancing at my watch, I stared in bug-eyed wonderment at this run-and-gun battle. In four action-packed minutes, I counted thirty-one dives at the coyote by the defending pair of hawks.

Completely flustered and confused by the ongoing cooperative and synchronized attack, the coyote was now running full out, nervously glancing overhead. The fracas had taken the combatants completely away from the hawks' nest and nearly out of their territory. The hawks had won the duel for today, and the danger at their nest was past, but there would be other days and other challenges, some less fortunate for the ferruginous hawks.

Little did I know then that I would again watch these enemies do deadly battle as I continued my three-year study of this desert hawk. But at this moment my hand, still shaking a tad in residual exhilaration, hastily scrawled the field notes of my first eye-witness account of the age-old feud. What had begun as just another tedious evening of observations and note-taking had certainly ended with a bang! That day, I might have titled my field notes "Hawks-1, Coyotes-0." But in truth I was too new to the ferruginous hawk's game of life and survival to dare to keep score. That would come later.

2

The Ferrug—inous—what?

F ew people have heard of the ferruginous
hawk, and fewer still have seen this bird. Such
anonymity is unfortunate, since this large raptor is strikingly beautiful. Its common name discour-
ages familiarity, simply because it is unfamiliar and
difficult to pronounce. Although its common name
appears to make little sense, its Latin meaning actually makes a lot of sense. "Ferruginous" refers to the
rusty color that appears prominently on the hawk's
shoulders and thighs, and sometimes is sprinkled
over parts of the tail and underbody.

However, those who know this hawk in a more
technical way are aware that its scientific name more
closely mirrors its true character: *Buteo regalis*, the
regal or majestic hawk. This beautiful rusty-and-
white desert hawk, perched atop a juniper, is guar-
anteed to grab your attention.

In the beginning, it was merely scientific curiosity that led me to select this bird as the object of my
studies for my Ph.D. dissertation at Idaho State University. I'd only seen this hawk twice in my life and
hardly knew enough about the bird for an intelli-
gent discussion. The ferruginous hawk certainly was
not a "political icon" like the peregrine falcon, bald
eagle or, later on, the spotted owl. Consequently,

there was little interest, incentive or funding available to support my study. Only the species' anonymity and unknown status throughout the West fostered the slightest and purely nominal interest by wildlife agencies.

Yet, armed with only a small grant from the Frank M. Chapman Fund (American Museum of Natural History), and the blessings of my graduate advisor, I began a three-year labor of love, investigating the nesting behavior of the ferruginous hawk in southern Idaho. I was a greenhorn raptor biologist, and knew from the very beginning that the learning curve was going to be really steep. I just didn't realize how steep.

Ironically, one big incentive for studying this desert hawk was the blatant lack of information about the species. That factor was more attractive than discouraging, since doctoral research, by definition, must provide original data. The little existing information about this hawk in the scientific literature was fairly vague and based largely on scattered accounts dating back nearly a century. More recent studies were practically non-existent, although a couple of new studies, like mine, were just getting underway in Colorado and Utah.

As I poked around in the literature accounts, and talked with a few biologists who had attempted to study the ferruginous hawk, it became increasingly obvious to me why there was such a dearth of nesting information on this bird. These attempts to study the nesting habits of ferruginous hawks shared a common fate. They had ended abruptly when the adult birds abandoned the nest. Obviously, nesting territories suddenly deserted by resident hawks had little to offer biologists.

The standard procedure for nesting studies is to survey suitable habitat to locate active nests, then climb into the nests periodically to collect data on food habits and the number of eggs laid or nestlings hatched. These periodic nest checks also provide other important facts, such as egg-laying dates, hatching dates, incubation periods and information on the young birds' success at fledging from the nest.

Surveys like these were an especially common study technique in the early days of raptor biology and, despite their intrusive nature, they were and are tolerated by most raptor species. But not the ferruginous hawk! This species is extremely sensitive to disturbance, especially when the birds are on their nest laying and incubating their eggs. A single visit at this time may lead to total nest abandonment by some hawks. This propensity nipped many a good ferruginous hawk study project in the bud, and most likely accounted for the notable lack of nesting behavior data on this species.

My study goals were profoundly tempered by this realization. The objective of my graduate research was to fill that void and to do so without disrupting my subjects' nesting cycle—an ambitious goal for a neophyte biologist. Yet, I felt I had sniffed out the reason for others' failures: untimely intrusion was the hawk's bane. Forearmed with that vital clue, I hoped I just might be able to transcend the boundaries of that sensitive inner circle of privacy in ferruginous hawk-dom. If so, a treasure trove of its life secrets would be mine for the discovery.

Yet another intriguing question surrounded the ferruginous hawk, although I was too naïve to be aware of it. The perceptive wisdom of Dr. Chuck Trost, my graduate advisor, put me onto this problem, which concerned the physiology of the birds' body-temperature control. That is, how do the nestlings of this large desert hawk manage to survive the scorching heat of the sun while exposed to it day after day in their typically large, open, and unshaded nests?

Whether these nests were in their usual place atop squat junipers, or on the ground or the open bluffs of desert foothills, this raptor was truly a hawk in the sun. This question of heat-stress survival by young ferruginous hawks seemed notably pertinent in light of the mounting and disturbing evidence of occasional heat-stress related deaths of young golden eagles throughout the western United States. Thus, under Chuck Trost's tutelage, I determined also to scrutinize this desert hawk's thermoregulatory adaptations for survival —in other words, find out how baby ferruginous hawks manage to survive the desert heat.

3

The Search is On

The first big question for me was could I, and where would I, find enough ferruginous hawks (or "ferrugs," as I came to call them) to provide several nests for study sites? So uncertain was the status of this hawk that there was little helpful information on the whereabouts of an ample population. Consequently, much of my first summer of research was spent exploring potential habitat in the southeastern Idaho desert in search of ferrugs.

While assisting others on bird studies in the Curlew Valley, I had occasionally noticed ferruginous hawks. So my search started there and then spread to the neighboring large, juniper-strewn expanses of Black Pine Valley and parts of Raft River Valley bordering Utah. These valleys, once bays of prehistoric glacial Lake Bonneville, open to the south onto its remnant, the Great Salt Lake Basin. Bordered mostly by juniper and sagebrush foothills, the valley floors, each several miles wide, were mostly taken up by scattered livestock ranches and agricultural development. In spring, they were carpeted with miles of greenery nurtured by melting snow and vernal rains. Then the desert landscape pleased the eye, but as summer commenced, the scene quickly changed. Shades of brown shimmered in the heat waves and powder dust boiled up behind my car along the back roads I traveled in search of this elusive hawk.

In this backcountry, I never tired of the tangy aroma of sagebrush and juniper, or the ever-present singing of meadowlarks. Every day was full of wildlife sightings. As I scoured portions of this countryside on foot, the frequent startling burst of a jackrabbit from beneath its favorite clump of sagebrush or greasewood held promise of an ample food supply for the hawk I hunted. Ferrugs seemed to be attracted mostly to the valley margins, where grass-shrub communities were bordered by scattered, low-growing junipers. In fact, it quickly became evident that this species would be found only along the lower edge of the juniper communities where, even there, they preferred the more isolated trees that stood as lone sentinels overlooking adjoining sagebrush flats.

This edge-like transition habitat, where the juniper forest met the open sagebrush flats, is known by ecologists as an "ecotone." This word refers to the place where two very different habitats abut and begin to grade from one to the other. I quickly discovered that the ferruginous hawk is an ecotone species.

The juniper tree used by the ferrugs in this part of Idaho is the Utah juniper (*Juniperus osteosperma*). It is shorter and bushier than the taller, spire-shaped species found elsewhere in the state. Consequently, several nests I found in these squat but sturdy junipers were barely more than head high.

The junipers are tough little trees. And being low-grown, their gnarled, stout branches made it quite easy for me to ascend to check the crown for a prospective nest site. Only once throughout my entire study did I grab onto a juniper branch that suddenly broke and sent me sprawling to the ground flat on my back. I was thankful for the absence of rocks or, worse yet, cactus beneath the tree that might have made for a treacherous landing. As it was, all I suffered was momentary deflation of my lungs and slight injury to my pride. Perhaps I was temporarily dazed, but I think I heard hawks chuckling in the distance.

The ferruginous hawk's large size is reflected in the bulk of its nest. I quickly learned to recognize the birds' huge stick nests, which occupied juniper tops. Even the sticks comprising the nests are larger than those used by other hawk species living in the area, such as red-tailed or Swainson's. During nest construction, it was not unusual to see ferruginous hawks on the ground, picking up large, old weathered pieces of sagebrush, sometimes grasping them in their talons and yanking them from the ground with powerful wingbeats. Most of the sticks were carried in by the male hawk, while the female spent her time arranging them, then adding softer material for the nest cup lining, often fine bark she stripped from nearby juniper branches.

Ferrugs spend an inordinate amount of time and energy building their nests. Three years of close observation during this stage of the nesting season taught me that nest building by the mated pair likely serves double duty. It results in a sturdy nest, but it is also an important pair-bonding and courtship activity. Therefore, it is not too surprising that ferrugs end up with nests that are large and substantial enough to sometimes entice the much larger golden eagles to use them in subsequent years. Newly constructed nests often end up being three to four feet across and one to two feet deep. In addition, it is quite common for the same nest to be reused by the same pair of hawks over the years, or by other raptors during intervening years. As you might expect, this continued use of the same nest, year after year, continues to add to its bulk.

I recall a ferruginous hawk nest I once found in an old, dead juniper tree. It obviously had been active a long time, until a new interstate highway was constructed through the birds' territory. Of course, the freeway put an abrupt end to their use of it. (Remember that this hawk is extremely sensitive to disturbance early in its nesting season.) That nest was one of the largest I had ever seen, but I was even more impressed with the two additional, huge piles of sticks on the ground below; sticks that had fallen from the nest over long years of use. I would guess that tree had been occupied by nesting ferrugs for half a century or more before the highway's intrusion.

Even the ground nests built by ferruginous hawks are impressively large in size. Early records in Utah describe ground nests six feet tall and nine feet across. The existence of ground nests raises the question: Aren't they at the mercy of coyotes, foxes, bobcats, and badgers? How this desert hawk manages to survive the many perils of ground nesting became increasingly apparent to me during the three years of my study.

Although most nests in my study area were in juniper trees, ferruginous hawks nest in a variety of places. One of the more fascinating aspects of this trait is the ferrugs' capacity to locate its large nest directly on the ground as well as on the more typical elevated sites such as broad-leaf trees, cliffs, utility poles, out-buildings, or even haystacks or windmills. Not only do ferrugs nest on different substrates, they also use a diversity of nesting material.

A century ago, U.S. Army Captain Charles E. Bendire described ground nests on the Great Plains that incorporated bleached buffalo bones. These nests first caught his attention when he noticed conspicuous circles of bones scattered across the prairie. At first he didn't know quite what to make of them. Later, he discovered they were the remains of ferrug nests, left after prairie fires had consumed the stick portions. Today, raptor biologists believe conspicuous splashes of white defecation around some raptor aeries likely function as important "flags" or advertisements of nest status or occupation. I often have wondered if those conspicuous white "rings of bones" served as important sign stimuli to attract passing ferrugs to traditional nest sites and territories.

Amid the jumble of expected sticks and sagebrush stalks, I occasionally discovered oddities in the ferrug nests I looked into: pieces of barbed wire, deer antler, baling twine, cardboard chunks, plastic, and even dried cow dung.

As time went on during my first year of study, I learned to recognize regions of suitable habitat for ferruginous hawks. Then it was just a matter of focusing my efforts on those prospective sectors of the valleys. After many days in the field, I located more than forty active nests.

Because of the shy and retiring nature of this hawk species, much of my study had to be conducted from concealed observation points or "blinds." I began my observations cautiously at only two or three nests that first year. Then, over the next two years, I intensified my observations and also used time-lapse photography equipment at selected nest sites to record additional nesting behavior. These efforts, which entailed moving in close enough to learn many little-known details of ferrug behavior, had to be conducted with excruciating caution to avoid disturbing the sensitive birds. The challenges were legion, and sometimes exhausting, but the adventures and triumphs of surmounting them remain forever etched in my heart, and certainly molded a kinship with this desert hawk.

Rich Howard, an active falconer, previously had trained and flown a ferruginous hawk for a period of time. After he heard I was beginning a study on ferrugs along the Idaho/Utah border, he drove out to my study area and introduced himself. After tagging along in the field with me for several days, Rich, too, quickly became enamored with the prospects of studying this species.

At first, I didn't know quite what to make of Rich's interest in my research, but he was pleasant company and a great deal of help, so we continued to work together. However, Rich soon announced he wanted to become part of my research project! It was obvious that our fieldwork together had fanned into flames a latent passion for ferrugs and stirred in Rich the prospect of studying them. Unfortunately, this created an awkward and increasingly uncomfortable research situation. I had begun the project as a quest of my own research, which had to be original and mine alone, in order to satisfy the requirements for a Ph.D. Now my personal research objectives would have to be divided somehow and portions forfeited to Rich.

After mulling the situation over in my mind, I discussed it at some length with Dr. Trost. We agreed the matter needed to be resolved, and the sooner the better. The three of us—Rich, Chuck Trost and I—held an intense meeting. Discussing various aspects of ferruginous hawk research that might be pursued, we sorted out what each of us would do and still not encroach on the other's study topics. In the end, I decided to concentrate strictly on nesting behavior and thermoregulatory (body temperature) research. Rich would proceed to study nesting ecology, including things like egg clutch size, hatching and fledging success, food habits and size differences between sexes.

In retrospect, this division of labor was probably one of the best things that could have happened to me. I had more than enough work to handle just concentrating on the nesting behavior aspects of the ferruginous hawk. Rich and I amiably continued our cooperative efforts through the second summer, lending each other helping hands and sharing pertinent information.

4

Camera Shy

Studying such a shy, easily disturbed hawk soon instilled within me a near reverence for the sanctity of hawk nests—they were to be regarded as a sacred trust of sorts. My every move around these nests was cautiously planned with the safeguarding and well-being of the hawks foremost in mind. I placed my observation blinds only at considerable distance from the nests, usually 100 yards or more; the earlier in the nesting season, the farther away.

The process of placing the blinds itself was tedious. The step-by-step procedure took me nearly two weeks. First, I would carry in the unassembled pieces of the blind and quickly lay them in a small, inconspicuous pile on the ground at the pre-selected site well away from the nest. Retreating to a point a long distance from the nest, I then watched the resident hawks for several hours to make sure they returned to the nest and resumed their normal activity. When I was satisfied that all was well, I allowed the hawks time to accept this new "foreign" object lying at the edge of their territory. After two to three days, I again entered the territory, quickly assembled the blind into its erect position, then beat a hasty retreat, observing the hawk's reaction from a distance, again making certain they accepted the structure.

After allowing another several days for them to get used to the presence of the assembled blind, I felt it safe to finally visit the blind for my first observation period. As an added precaution, I entered the blind before daylight in order to minimize disturbance to the hawks. Once inside my blind, hidden from view of the hawks, I recorded their nesting activities with as little disruption as possible to their daily routine. Later in the day, when I left the blind after several hours of observation, I would exit quickly and walk away as directly as possible. Viewing the hawks' activity from this distance, even with a spotting scope, revealed only broad, general nesting activity to me. I soon became frustrated with my limited ability to see the detailed behavior of the most intimate interactions of the adults and nestlings. Somehow, I needed to obtain a closer look at the life of the ferruginous hawk. In fact, the best means for recording such detailed behavior would be photographically—but how? Especially with this easily spooked species and particularly on a practically non-existent research budget? Oh, the challenges!

I did about the only thing possible. With part of my meager grant money, I obtained a couple of inexpensive 8-mm movie cameras capable of taking single frame, time-lapsed pictures. These cameras were designed to click off a frame at one-half- to five-minute intervals. If I could position them close enough to two hawk nests, they would record the details of the birds' activities that I needed—even while I worked elsewhere on my project. The trick, of course, would be to set up the cameras near the nests without spooking the hawks. A difficult trick—

but if successful, a veritable information trove awaited me!

If a mere untimely visit to a ferruginous hawk nest could upset the birds enough that they would abandon their territory, how could I hope to successfully install a photography contraption close enough to an active nest to record detailed activity? That question plagued me for days as I assembled my camera gear.

I was learning ferruginous hawk behavior with every step I took to move in close to them. For everything I did within a nesting territory, I first had to learn how much the residents would tolerate—without crowding them to the point of nest desertion. It was like a delicate chess game, pitting my research needs against the hawks' tolerance, or lack thereof. I wanted to weave together an understanding of their daily life at the nest, but I vowed to do so without unraveling their delicate avian psyches. In order to sleuth out their secrets of survival, I needed to dissect their behavior, but I was determined to do so without murdering my subjects. From the beginning to the end of my study, every day was a learning experience—and I loved it!

For my first experiment with the time-lapse cameras, I decided to mount one in a juniper about eight yards from one of the nest trees. The camera was housed inside an Army-surplus metal ammunition box. A glass-covered window had been cut in both ends. To make this foreign contraption less obvious to the hawks, I camouflaged the outside of the ammo box with juniper branches so it blended into its surroundings. Connected by wires to a car battery buried in a box at the base of the tree, this unit caused no problems with the hawks and functioned for several weeks until cattle trampled in the top of the battery box.

Naturally, since I was working with the "poster child" for species sensitive to disturbance, I had to be very cautious in positioning the camera anywhere near the hawk nest. I used a gradual procedure, as I did to place blinds. First, I wired a small "foreign bundle" of juniper branches in the eventual camera spot. Again, I retreated to see if this disturbed the hawks. I followed this with a larger bundle of sticks several days later. Next, I put the actual camera box in place but did not activate the camera. Only when the hawks appeared to accept this did I start the camera and finally begin recording nesting behavior. I still wasn't certain what image quality to expect from this set-up, but at least it had better potential than my distance viewing from blinds. I was just thankful for any means for getting a close-up look at behavior at the hawk nest. And, thus far, it had been accomplished with no harm done to the nesting hawks.

I was eager to get my second camera in place for similar data collection. The problem was, very few other nests had "tripod trees" conveniently located nearby. At the best candidate, the nearest I could set up a time-lapse camera was thirty-two yards from the nest tree. Since the cameras didn't have good telephoto capabilities, I worried that the results would be too poor at that distance. The first roll of film I developed from that set-up justified my fears. The camera had to be much closer to the nest to record clear details of behavior, especially that of the young hawks. But that would just about mandate placing cameras in the nest trees themselves, and I knew that would be risky business with ferruginous hawks. Recall that the junipers in my study area were small, squat trees, without a lot of room in which to work. Would the hawks stand for the intrusion of a camera box in the same tree as their nest? I knew of only one way to find out—I had to try it!

My fears were soon realized. To minimize the danger of causing nest abandonment, I did not attempt to install a camera in a nest tree until after young were hatched. None the less, my first placement of a camera in one of the nest trees disturbed the adults enough that they were reluctant to return to the nest and remained away throughout most of the day. Although the male made two or three food deliveries to the nest, the female never returned to butcher the prey and feed the young, her normal behavior. Rich and I waited, agonized, hoping above hope that the female's caution would yield to the stronger, age-old urge to care for her chicks. But apparently the camouflaged camera box was just too much of an intrusive unknown for the hawks' comfort. By sundown, the female still had not returned to her nest. We had to intervene!

Hastening to the nest tree, we climbed into the nest and found that one chick had perished, apparently from exposure and/or lack of food. The two remaining chicks had empty crops, were extremely cold and were barely able to move. I left the dead chick in the nest overnight, hoping that its presence might discourage total nest abandonment by the adults. With Rich's help, I removed the camera along with the two remaining chicks, which we kept overnight for rehabilitation at the nearby field station quarters. On the way there, Rich drove while I held the cold, moribund chicks under my shirt against my belly to warm them. By the time we arrived, I could feel the downy little bodies beginning to move and squirm more and more against my tummy, as they emitted plaintive little peeps.

We quickly assembled a small, padded cardboard box, placed the chicks inside it and set them on a shelf above our gas cook stove for warmth. By watching the chicks' activity, we were able to regulate the temperature for their comfort. Although they seemed momentarily out of danger from the cold, we were also concerned about their apparent lack of food that day. So leaving the bundled chicks in the warmth of their box, we made a mercy run into the sagebrush-covered countryside and shot a jackrabbit for emergency hawk food. We returned to our quarters and force-fed small amounts of jackrabbit and decarbonated Coca-Cola to the chicks at intervals throughout the night. The reason for the flat soda was not so much that "things go better with Coke," but rather to contribute needed fluid, glucose and electrolytes to their diet.

After the long night's vigil, we were relieved to find that by morning the chicks showed signs of complete recovery. Shortly after dawn we returned the bright-eyed and perky chicks to the nest and removed their dead nest mate. Within the hour the adult female ferruginous hawk returned to the nest, fed and brooded her two returned "abductees," We deeply regretted the loss of the chick but we were greatly relieved that at least we had salvaged the nesting effort and life at that site was now back to normal.

Weeks later, when Rich and I returned to that nest and banded those now big, strapping nestlings before they fledged, I think we both looked upon them with an extra tinge of paternal affection, recalling our near-heroic efforts to revive them that chilly, spring night.

As it happened, three years later, I opened an official letter from the Bird Banding Laboratory and read that one of these rescued nestlings had perished in Mexico during its long, perilous migratory journey. Its band had been turned into wildlife authorities, who then alerted us to its fate. With the help of a translator, I sent a letter to the person in Mexico who had turned in the hawk's band and requested further information.

Rather promptly, I received a letter neatly penned in Spanish by a lad who lived on a ranch in Mexicali, Baja California. In his letter he reported in proud naivete how he had encountered this rather tame "eagle" and was able to approach it close enough to shoot it. His words stung as though they had been shot from his gun! Unmindful of the atrocity he had committed, he dutifully reported the band number and colored wing-tags found on the bird.

Because of the hawk's special story in my life, I felt a personal touch of sadness at that bit of news. My mind was re-visited by the memory of that bitter-cold day when those downy little chicks were wiggling against my bare stomach during our rescue mission as they struggled to survive. They both had cheated death once. Who knows how many other narrow escapes they had had later. And now, one of them had lost its final confrontation—with a bullet. Even though it is common knowledge among biologists that more than two-thirds of young birds never live to see their second year, I personally grieved for that particular one.

5

Penelope,
the Stay-at-Home Mom

As the third and final summer of my study approached, I found myself with conflicting feelings. On the one hand, I was feeling comfortable around ferruginous hawks and was confident that I knew the species probably as well as anyone in all of North America. I was glad I had maintained my soft-touch approach to their study, and with painstaking care had forged so many fragile accords with the eight nesting pairs I had under surveillance.

Although from time to time I had unknowingly courted disaster with these sensitive hawks, as yet the only harm I was aware I had done them was the single chick's mortality. Maybe I had just been lucky, but I think maintaining a healthy respect for their need for solitude and space contributed to my success. In a sense, I was loathe to infringe upon a trust I had painstakingly forged with this desert hawk— perhaps risking serious consequences.

On the other hand, I was feeling pressure to know more about their behavior than I had been able to observe from a distance, and time was running out. Although I had been able to record a considerable amount of nesting behavior from my blinds, it was only general information on overall nesting dynamics because the hawks' aura of vulnerability had held me somewhat at bay; their touchiness to human encroachment had kept me from crowding them too closely. About to begin my final year of research, I still lacked an opportunity for close-range, direct observation at nest sites. I also needed a way to make good, close-up 35mm photographs of detailed behaviors—with the limited technology in those days, even time-lapse photography had provided only a few snatches of fairly close-up documentation. In particular, I had to be closer to the birds in order to observe and document the thermoregulatory behaviors the hawks employed to survive heat stress. In short, I desperately needed a ferruginous hawk that would allow me to get "up close and personal" for a more intimate look at life at the nest.

Lacking that, however, I was otherwise prepared. In order to gather body temperature data, I had obtained a receiver and a pair of miniature temperature-sensitive radio transmitters ("Mini-mitters") that would record the daily body temperatures of young hawks as they sat in their nests through the heat of the day. I had no precedent to follow in this experimental technique; I was charting new ground. The mini-mitters were a little over an inch long, about the diameter of a pencil, and were temperature-sensitive. All I had to do was to force-feed them to the baby hawks as soon as they were large enough to comfortably swallow one.

I hoped the chicks would retain their mini-mitters for about twenty-four hours and then cast up or regurgitate them along with other matter in pellets or "castings." This ejection of indigestible fur, feathers, and bones is a common daily practice for virtually all birds of prey, even young ones. While they remained inside the baby hawks, the mini-mitters would transmit continuous beep-like signals to the receiver. These signals would fluctuate directly with the birds' body temperature, so I could monitor the chicks' body temperatures throughout the day from a nearby blind. If my blind was at close range, I could also view and record the behavioral responses of the heat-stressed chick.

The plan was great, but it all hinged on my being able to move to within twenty-five or thirty yards of the monitored nest, the optimal range at which I could pick up the mini-mitter signals on my receiver. That is very close to a ferruginous hawk nest, especially since I would have to start my observations when the chicks were only ten days old. With memories of the time-lapse camera fiasco still fresh in my mind, I knew I was facing my greatest research challenge.

One slim possibility of success kept flitting into my mind. It involved a unique individual female ferruginous hawk I had come to know in the past two summers, when I often had pondered my chances of moving in close to one of the nests.

One of the first things a naturalist learns about members of wildlife populations is that they express a lot of individuality. Often, it's their appearance. However, behaviors in individuals sometimes border on "personality" traits. One particular female ferruginous hawk in my study had personality!

She nested on the southwest fringe of the Wildcat Hills, south of Snowville, Utah. Both years when I visited her nest to band her nestlings, I had been impressed by her apparent tameness. She was aggressive enough and dove on me several times each visit, but soon would land on a nearby tree and content herself with simply screaming at me. I noticed her on my first visit because of the great photo opportunities she presented from that perch—the best "Kodak moment" any ferruginous hawk had yet provided. After a repeat performance on my second visit the next year, I dubbed her "Penelope." Like the wife of Odysseus who, during his absence, kept her many suitors at bay by faithfully remaining in her home under the pretense of weaving a shroud. Penelope the hawk exhibited a close bond to her home and would sit close by, even when I intruded into her nest.

With her unusually tame behavior in mind, I wondered if Penelope might tolerate a close-up blind—if I worked it into her inner territory prudently. The more I thought about it, the more convinced I became that she was my best chance for a truly intimate and comprehensive look at life in a ferruginous hawk nest.

Early the third spring, my plans were complete. But would they succeed? I fought back the recurring, nagging fear that I wouldn't find Penelope back at her nest again. What if the many perils of that little-known black hole of migration and wintering had snuffed out her life? Then what would I do? I considered the possibilities at other territories; none held the promise of Penelope's nest.

Mid-May rolled around. It was time to check Penelope's territory to see if she had returned to nest again. Heading for the Wildcat Hills that morning with some trepidation, I was glad for the company of a newfound field partner. Rich had completed his research the previous year and was gone. However, I was fortunate to gain a new research companion. Tim Craig, a colleague of mine, asked to tag along with me to learn a little about the raptors of southern Idaho. Tim's 6' 6" slender, well-muscled frame added considerable prowess to my fieldwork capabilities that summer.

At first, I feared that Tim wouldn't like roughing it for days at a time in the desert of southern Idaho and northern Utah. Fortunately, he took an immediate liking to all things wild and we quickly became the best of friends.

On our way into the Wildcat Hills late that morning in 1974, my mind was mercifully diverted from concerns about Penelope's return by the more immediate challenge of keeping my vehicle safely on the ridges of the deeply rutted road. I was hugging the steering wheel of my little V-W squareback, doing my usual Mario Andretti impression to avoid the ruts. Many of these old desert roads were challenging, since I didn't have much clearance with my little car and could easily get high-centered—a long way from help! We seldom encountered other drivers out in this remote country—maybe a coyote hunter or an occasional rancher looking for lost livestock—and I usually went several days without seeing other travelers, especially here in the Wildcat Hills. Grimly intent on the furrowed road, I could detect the whites of Tim's eyes to my side; he was just getting acquainted with these cow-path, back-country tracks. (On occasion, these roads did, indeed, evaporate into a cowpath.)

It was one of those late-spring days in the high desert when the weather seemed unable to make up its mind. Intermittent sunshine had warmed our spirits when we left Snowville less than an hour earlier. Now, as we neared the juniper-fringed hills, dark clouds rolled low overhead and spitting snow dulled the verdant green of the surrounding shrub-grass landscape. Only scattered clumps of bright pink phlox and clusters of bluebonnet reassured us of the lateness of the season. As I slowed my car to a stop, a quarter-mile from Penelope's territory, sunshine already was mocking the futile efforts of the departing snow squall. I rested my spotting scope on my car window to see if I could resolve the question that had been burning in my mind for months—had Penelope returned?

It was the moment of truth and I didn't like what I was seeing: nothing! I quickly scanned Penelope's nest tree and many of the surrounding junipers. A faint specter of dread began to tighten its grip on my throat. I swallowed hard. "Let's go in on foot and check it out," I said to Tim. "I can't find anything through the scope!" I was fighting back sickening disappointment.

Though the nest tree was in the open and easily seen, from our angle the view of the nest itself was partially obscured by branches. As we strolled into the territory, I still held onto a glimmer of hope that just maybe there was a hawk on the nest. Optimistically, I hoped at any moment for the comforting sight of an adult bird suddenly flaring up from the nest and out of the tree. However, hope withered with each step of our approach. Finally, we stopped a mere five yards from the tree. I was crushed.

"Obviously, nobody's home," I dejectedly observed to Tim. "I may as well climb the nest and see if its been worked on at —all—"

Before I could finish the sentence, a large female ferruginous hawk erupted from the nest and swooped by us, startling us both! She circled low overhead, watching us. I was elated!

"That's got to be Penelope!" I exclaimed, grinning at Tim. "Did you see how tight she stuck to that nest before she finally bailed out?"

In trademark Penelope fashion, this female ferruginous hawk had indeed remained on her nest until the very last minute. Had I not spoken, she might not have flown at all and we would have left the area totally unaware of her presence. Most ferrugs would have flown while we were yet fifty to one hundred yards away. Hidden so low in the nest before she flushed, she must still be incubating her eggs. That also pleased me, because it gave me a little more time to finalize my strategy; I wanted to have a blind in place near her nest soon after her eggs hatched.

Thus began my close association with this hawk —a unique association that steadily grew into a deep fascination and a naturalist's love for Penelope, the "stay-at-home mom"!

Penelope's mate delivering lizard prey at the nest

Two juvenile Ferruginous Hawks nearly old
enough to leave their nest

A young Ferruginous Hawk being weighed

Five to 7 day-old Ferruginous Hawk nestlings

Fledgling melanistic (dark form) Ferruginous
Hawk hunting in a field

Day's end at a Ferruginous Hawk nest - reprieve
from the searing afternoon temperatures

6

Stumbling Onto A Ground Nest

While waiting for Penelope's eggs to hatch so I could more safely move a blind in close, I literally stumbled onto another golden study opportunity. One of the persistent frustrations of my study had been my inability to locate an active ground nest of a ferruginous hawk. I desperately wanted to set up a blind and make some comparisons between the nesting behavior of the hawks at tree nests and ground nests. The increased vulnerability of ground nesting had me curious. How do these birds manage to successfully pull that off? Do they operate differently than tree nesters?

Although I had found one active ground nest during the first year of my study, it had not been re-occupied. All of the others I had happened onto were old and unused. The only other ground nests I was aware of were located a couple hundred miles to the north, in the Arco desert. The logistics of trying to jockey between these two widely separated study areas was daunting, especially in light of the recent energy crisis that had just sent gas prices sky-rocketing. My "shoe-string" research budget certainly couldn't absorb the extra expense.

After confirming Penelope's return, a few days later I drove on around the northwest fringe of the Wildcat Hills, checking out other ferruginous hawk territories that had been active in the past. One nest was occupied but the other appeared to be vacant. I continued on around the north end of the Wildcat Hills and soon spotted another ferruginous hawk soaring high over a treeless stretch of rolling foothills. As I watched this bird it suddenly descended out of sight behind a distant hill farther to the east. I motored on along the dusty little road I was traveling until a distant, narrow lip of rimrock came into view off to the south, where the soaring hawk had just disappeared. I had never noticed the rock outcrop before. I studied it for a time through the scope and wondered if it might be a likely place for a ferruginous hawk ground nest. The closest approach was on foot but to do that I'd first need to backtrack along the road a couple of miles. From there, I could hike directly over the backside of the little cliff from the west.

Retracing my path along the dusty road, I found a spot where the vegetation was low enough to pull off the road, parked and struck out on foot across the sagebrush foothills bound for the distant small escarpment. Soon, the brushy terrain began a gradual rise to the hilltop where I estimated the rock face to be. Topping the rise, I began searching for the rock I had spied earlier. Then it happened! As I rounded a little knob at the top, I was startled as a large white hawk sprang off its nest, which now loomed into view on the edge of the rocky lip, a mere ten yards in front of me. I had unwittingly blundered directly onto an active ferruginous hawk ground nest

—something I had earnestly sought for the past two years!

In a mixed stroke of luck I had at once made a sterling discovery and at the same time had committed the unpardonable sin against the ferruginous hawk: intruding on an incubating female at the very time when she is most intolerant of disturbance. To make matters worse, I had surprised the bird as I burst in upon her unexpectedly, further exacerbating my blunder. Rich and I had decided long ago that it seemed better to make resident birds well aware of our presence before nearing the nest. We both felt that giving the territorial bird fair warning of our approach was probably less stressful on the hawks, and more importantly, allowed them a more casual departure with less chance of accidentally dislodging eggs or downy young from the nest.

Chagrined by my blunder, I immediately retreated, noticing as I left that the female hawk had quit circling and calling overhead and had dropped down to a bare patch of ground in the sagebrush flat 150 yards to the east. As I hiked back to my car, I kept replaying the scenario over in my mind. On one hand, I was jubilant over my discovery, but on the other, I bemoaned the bad fortune of my unannounced arrival. Back at my vehicle, I quickly drove back to the east where I could keep the nest under surveillance with my spotting scope and watch for the return of the female hawk.

I found a little higher vantage point nearby and from there could make out the white figure of the female hawk in the distance, still perched out in the sage east of the nest. I waited and watched, hoping that any minute she would leave her ground perch and return to the nest and eggs. It was a pleasant day with intermittent sunshine, so I wasn't too concerned about the exposed eggs chilling or overheating. My primary fear was that the female hawk might have been so traumatized by my intrusion that she wouldn't return to her nest. During all this, I noted the absence of the male hawk, even while the female had circled overhead calling in defense. However, this was not entirely unusual. After all, the males were often out hunting, sometimes at great distances from the nest and for long periods of time.

Anxiously I continued to await the outcome of my homemade crisis. Then hope suddenly shimmered in the distance. It was the whitish form of a ferruginous hawk, flying in toward the nest from the southeast. It wasn't the female. She was still at her ground perch. The male hawk, apparently arriving with food, sailed down onto the nest and perched at its edge. This would be a telling moment. Would the female now return to the nest to receive the gift of food from her mate? Or was she still too unsettled from my visit to return? A minute elapsed before the female launched off the ground and, to my jubilation, winged her way back to the nest, where she perched with the male. The male ferrug soon departed, and so did I, greatly relieved and rejoicing over my good fortune.

On my way from the ground nest that day, I discovered a short-cut back to the main highway. In the future, it could provide more direct and much quicker access to the ground nest from my Snowville base camp. One minor hitch to the short cut, however, was that a stretch of the dirt road traversed a sector of fenced, private land. There, the road was gated at the fence line but the gate was not padlocked so I motored on through to the highway at the far end of the property. That was where I noticed the "keep out" signs near the exit gate. Obviously, if I planned to use this road to access the ground nest, I would need to obtain permission to enter this area. It usually wasn't a problem gaining access to these posted areas. Overall, I'd found the landowners friendly and quite cooperative—for the most part, they just wanted to know your reason for being there. The real problem, more often, was finding out who the heck owned the property since, as in this case, there might not be a ranch house within miles. I'd inquire about this route when I got back to Snowville.

"Oh, that chunk of land belongs to ol' Greasy. He lives a ways further down the highway...lives in an old school bus!" I was later informed by the amiable gas station owner in Snowville. I tried to pin down a more formal name for this school bus-occupying landowner, but to no avail.

"Naw, he just goes by Greasy, you'll understand when you see 'im," the gas station owner insisted, with the faintest hint of a twinkle in his eye.

So the next day, on our way out to the Wildcat Hills, Tim and I paid a social call on the man called "Greasy," at his school bus abode. I was hoping to find him at home and also find him amenable to my crossing his property on my way to and from the recently discovered ground nest. Greasy's place was not difficult to spot along the highway. In fact, I'd noticed it before on previous trips and had been kind of curious about it.

His driveway was strewn with all manner of auto skeletons and piles of parts. The old yellow school bus looked to be some mutated hybrid of home and shop. In the shade of a tattered canopy extending from the north side of the bus sat what at first glance appeared to be an African-American gazing in my direction, eating a peeled apple. I got out of my car, walked over and greeted him. Instantly, I realized that the "Negro" was actually a Caucasian heavily soiled from head to toe with well-established grease and grime. It didn't take rocket-science to figure out who this guy was. I was further astounded when the "apple" turned out to be a raw onion!

With dirty crew-cut hair, the general appearance of a chimney sweep and blood-shot eyes that, none-the-less, looked very white against his grimy face, Greasy chomped on his large, white onion with a smile as I explained my reason for stopping by. I don't recall the exact details of our conversation but he was friendly as he readily granted me permission to cross his land. I do remember being taken aback by his comment that, "A man who eats raw onions can't be worth a hell-of-a-lot!" Surprised, I lamely remarked that a man has the right to eat whatever he chooses! Greasy was indeed a colorful character, in more ways than one, and thereafter, our destination became affectionately known as the "Greasy ground nest."

The following week I returned to the Greasy ground nest area and watched from a distance using the spotting scope. Most of the ferruginous hawk eggs in the other nests in my study area had hatched by now and I was curious to know if that was also the case at the ground nest. Sure enough, as I watched, the female hawk raised herself up, shifted her position and made motions down in the nest as if feeding young. Anxious to begin my first ever observations at a ground nest, over the next five days I successfully worked a blind into position some sixty yards north of it. In addition, I also positioned a camouflaged, time-lapse camera near the top of the rocky knoll with a view into the nest. This was my one and only opportunity to record behavior at a ferruginous hawk ground nest and I was determined to maximize my data collection!

7

Disaster Strikes Thrice!

Before daylight on May 22, I made my way on foot through the sagebrush and entered my blind at 5:05 a.m.—the first day of observations at the ground nest. I had checked the time-lapse camera the day before and confirmed that all was well at the nest. By 5:21 a.m., meadowlarks were beginning to sing, and I could make out the dark form of the female hawk on the nest facing into the dawn. Her figure loomed large through my thirty-power spotting scope. Even in the faint light, I could make out details as she maintained her alert vigil: quick head movements, an occasional blinking of her eyes, feathers on her shoulder and back ruffled by the light morning breeze. I imagined how warm and cozy her three downy chicks must feel beneath her and momentarily noticed the morning chill within my blind.

A few minutes later she shifted her position so she was now facing away from me toward the south, and began preening her back feathers. Periodically she stopped and glanced briefly around the area, alert. She was on the lookout for danger, no doubt, but perhaps also was anticipating a food delivery from her mate.

I had been observing the nest for nearly forty-five minutes now and the female had shuffled a little in the nest again but continued to preen over one shoulder or the other. Keeping her under surveillance through the spotting scope, I dictated the events of the morning into my tape recorder in periodic, low whispers. The sun had not quite cleared the mountains of the eastern horizon, yet it was nearly full light.

I had logged many such mornings in blinds at other hawk nests. The twilight of dawn always seems to whisper hope to the heart of a naturalist; to stir a sense of sacred timelessness, when the present seems to embrace antiquity. As I reveled in another tranquil dawn, I thought the sight before me—the hawk on her nest—would have been the same 10,000 years ago.

At 5:44 a.m., the female was in the midst of preening, when she suddenly jerked her head around. Simultaneously, she sprang to a standing position facing the southwest, flapped her wings and lashed out with taloned feet at the face of a coyote who, at that same instant, burst into view over the backside of the nest. The coyote stood its ground, dodging its head back to avoid the lethal, lashing feet of the female hawk as she instantly flared backward off the nest and flew off. She had barely cleared the nest when the coyote picked up one of the downy chicks and with a snap of its jaws, swallowed it. Immediately it picked up a second chick, chewed briefly, then gulped it down, too. Then, for some reason, the coyote disappeared from view behind the nest, only to reappear thirty seconds later. Back at the nest, the coyote ate the remaining chick and some prey remains at the nest, then walked a few steps toward my time-lapse camera box less than ten yards to the northwest. The canid then turned south and, like some surreal specter, vanished from view.

Inside my blind, I slumped in stunned silence. Antiquity had touched the present. What I had just witnessed had assuredly been played out thousands of times across these desert hills since time immemorial. My presence and witness, in this case, was merely a punctuation mark in the shrouded secrecy of the ongoing drama between these two predators. Had this event not occurred with such lightning speed, I might well have been tempted to explode out of my blind, screaming, "NOOOOOOOOOO!" On the other hand, my sole purpose for being there was to observe, to try and learn the intimate and natural details of the life of the ferruginous hawk and to do so with the least amount of participation and interference in those natural events.

I gathered my field gear and left the blind. Looking around for the female hawk, I spotted her sitting on the ground 150 yards to the east, facing the empty nest. As I stood and watched in numbed silence, she soon took to the air and flew slowly, low over her empty nest, then drifted off and disappeared in the distance to the southwest. I wondered what silent anthems played to her spirit in response to this tragically poignant moment in her life. As I watched her disappear from view I gifted her my shared feelings of sorrow. Trudging to the nest site, I dejectedly retrieved the time-lapse camera which, ironically, had malfunctioned and failed to record any of this incident. Disheartened by the events of the morning, I carried my equipment back to the car and headed back to the field station to relay the grim news to Tim.

As I drove out of the Wildcat Hills that morning, I remembered another scene that had shocked me barely a week earlier. Tim and I were checking on two nests over in the Raft River Valley that had potential for the placement of a blind. The nests were barely a quarter mile apart and, earlier that spring, I had been able to park my car between them and keep both nests under simultaneous observation. At one of these nests the female was a normal, light color, but the male hawk was melanistic, meaning he had very dark plumage. This made distinguishing between the sexes very easy. That spring I had learned much about the hawks' early territorial activity and nest-building behavior from watching those nests. Once they started incubation, I left them alone.

The other of the two nests had been named "Five Ferrug Nest" because these adults were a prolific pair and had produced five nestlings the first year of my study. This happens occasionally with this species but typically only during good food years, when jackrabbit numbers are at their peak. After that first year, the jackrabbit population had crashed and many of the original forty ferruginous hawk nests in my study area either became inactive or produced fewer young in the second and third years of my study.

This year, when we were sure the young had hatched, Tim and I went out to check on these two nests. As we neared the Five Ferrug Nest, I began looking for the adult female at her normal sentinel posts, either perched on the nest or nearby on the ground. Seeing nothing, I parked the car and we began walking to the nest, still scanning for the resident adults. As we drew closer, my heart sank. The nest was partly destroyed, with the edge of the big stick nest atop the squat, flat-topped juniper drooping. This was an obvious sign of predation. We inspected the damaged nest closely. It was somewhat out of kilter and empty. There was no sign of downy chicks, anywhere. The bottom of this nest was barely five feet high, and I could almost reach into it from the ground. The ground surrounding the nest was pockmarked with coyote tracks, but no signs of other possible disturbance.

Still mildly shocked by our discovery at the Five Ferrug Nest, we hurried over to the neighboring nest with the dark male, and again grew concerned when no adult hawks greeted our approach. At this nest we found even more evidence of nest destruction, with debris strewn down the tree to its base. Sticks littered the ground below. All that remained of the nest contents were a few remnant eggshells on the ground below the tree. Again, coyote tracks were scattered about the nest tree. It was pretty obvious that the same fate had befallen this nest, perhaps at about the same time.

Recalling these other recent coyote sagas while driving away from the ground nest debacle, my mind raced, juggling and regrouping my study options for the summer. Tragedy had struck thrice and I was beginning to feel totally pummeled by coyotes. What I was privileged to witness this morning at the ground nest sang out a timeless and telling refrain about life and death for the ferruginous hawk. Its chilling echo stirred me to the depths of my being. But somehow, just now, I did not feel privileged.

8

Eternal Enemies

In any wild natural habitat, different species are, due to their proximity or the respective roles they each play in the system, destined for conflict. So it seems to be with the ferruginous hawk and the coyote. The intense clashes I have described between the two species involved coyotes entering ferruginous hawk territories. Each invasion resulted in deadly conflict. However, my first observation of coyotes within a ferruginous hawk territory recorded a surprisingly benign response. The circumstances surrounding this interaction were somewhat different and may have accounted for the apparent lack of discord.

I was watching a ferruginous hawk nest in a juniper tree in the Blackpine Valley during midafternoon on April 1, 1972. This was another territory where the male was melanistic and easy to distinguish from the normal, light-colored female. The birds had been building a nest in a juniper but, as yet, did not appear to have laid eggs. As I watched the pair through a spotting scope from a distant back road, three coyotes appeared in the sagebrush and began to work their way by the hawks. Aside from preening, the hawks exhibited little, if any, concern.

Then the male flew to the female and copulated with her. Afterward, no other activity developed as the pair of hawks simply remained perched in the same tree. I watched for another hour but little else happened, aside from the female's flight to the nest tree and the coyotes' eventual disappearance from the territory.

I think each of my coyote-hawk observations differed enough in their circumstances to explain the variations in the hawks' responses and their very different outcomes. In the Blackpine Valley observation, the hawks were barely into the pre-incubation stage of the nesting season; they had no eggs or young to defend. Perhaps the incident of copulation was actually a low-intensity displacement/conflict behavior—a means of reducing aggression by the hawks in response to the threatening presence of the coyotes. Such behavior has been observed with snowy owls in similar, threatening circumstances.

Displacement behavior is performed in conflict situations when the animal is torn between alternative responses and consequently ends up doing something inappropriate for that situation. This is what is going on when people burst into nervous laughter in the midst of a very tense or grave situation. Then again, the coyotes were in full view of the hawks long before they approached the nest, removing the element of surprise by the intruders. Some or all of these factors may have played a part in the lack of any intense combat between the two species in this instance.

All of the other skirmishes I have observed between these two predators were fierce and potentially deadly, and they all occurred later in the nesting season when there were either eggs or young in the nest. The stakes were high for the hawks—the energy and investment they had put into their reproductive effort that season were on the line.

The single successful defense I observed against a coyote, which I described in the opening paragraphs of this book, was at a tree nest, and the hawks had several critical advantages. First, they detected the approaching predator early, so the birds were not surprised by the coyote. Second, both adults were on hand to execute a cooperative defense. In fact, the element of surprise was on the side of the hawks. Thirty-one alternating dives on the coyote with some striking the invader was a formidable defense, difficult for the coyote to parry. By contrast, the coyote encounter at the ground nest was fraught with disadvantages to the female hawk. She was surprised by the sudden presence of the coyote at the nest and had no opportunity to intercept the predator from the air, which might have diverted the coyote from the nest. Nor did she have assistance from her mate to help take the battle to the intruder, which raises the question: why was the male absent at the time of the coyote predation and when I first discovered the ground nest? This brings up a very critical and pertinent point regarding the whole dynamic between these eternal enemies, and I think the answer is based in ecology as much as behavior.

The low jackrabbit population throughout my study area in 1973 and 1974 made food harder to find and was reflected in the distant foraging patterns by male hawks. When males are forced to hunt far from home, female hawks are left alone to defend the nest between the male's food deliveries. The danger in this vulnerability is further compounded by the fact that the same scarcity of jackrabbits forces hungry coyotes to turn to alternative food sources, including young hawks. You can imagine the extreme danger ground-nesting hawks face during low-prey years, when coyotes are even successfully marauding nests in the lower-slung juniper trees. My observations that ground nests are active only during high jackrabbit densities may be a reflection of this vulnerability to hungry coyotes.

One of the things that struck me as I watched the coyote raid the ground nest was the coyote's apparent lack of concern with the adult female's presence. Instead, it was focused on the hapless chicks. Ignoring the female ferruginous hawk and directing its attention to gobbling up the nestlings suggested to me that the coyote was an experienced and proficient nest robber or starved, or perhaps both.

My observations of ferruginous hawk-coyote skirmishes were both daytime events. I expect that nocturnal raids by coyotes would be met with limited resistance from the adult hawks. This belief is again based upon my personal observations of ferruginous hawk behavior. On several occasions during both predawn and early nightfall periods while entering or leaving my observation blinds, I noticed little response from the resident hawks while I was near the nest or the male's night roost. These personal experiences lead me to believe the hawks don't see well in low light and don't muster much of a defense during nighttime raids.

One remaining factor regarding coyote predation at my ferruginous hawk nests needs to be confessed to. That is the role that I, the researcher, may have played each time that I visited them. It is the gritty reality every field researcher carries in the back of the mind as he or she knowingly lays down a scent trail to and from the nest with every visit, or makes the nest obvious because the adult hawks dive and scream at them. It is also the reason why every responsible researcher carefully considers the value of the information to be gained from that visit, and weighs it against the real likelihood that their visit will invite curious and ever-hungry terrestrial predators to the nest. Obviously, this is a particularly vital consideration with ground-nesting animals.

With all that in mind, from the very beginning I tried to limit my activity around ferruginous hawk nests to the bare essentials. Still, I wonder if I must shoulder some of the blame for some of the nest predations. My hope is that the information gained from my interlopings in ferruginous hawk territories has greatly outweighed the damage I have unintentionally caused.

9

Winged Marauders of the Night

Throughout my study I kept encountering evidence of another, more furtive mortal enemy of the ferruginous hawk. This particular enemy was a winged marauder that seemed fairly proficient at making occasional nocturnal raids on nests and successfully picking off a nestling.

But first one must appreciate the round-the-clock nature of the predatory drama that repeatedly unfolds within any little sector of the landscape. As evening shadows lengthen into nightfall, there is a subtle changing of the guard among raptors. This was vividly brought home to me one moonlit night while I sat out a strange and lonely vigil at a ferruginous hawk nest.

My reason for a moonlit watch was to see if these desert hawks ever hunted after dark. Following the jackrabbit population crash in my study area after the first season of my research, I noticed that kangaroo rats began showing up as prey items at several nests. If you've ever kept these rodents as pets, you soon discovered, to your dismay, that they're not much fun to watch during the daytime because they are nocturnal. I suspected that ferruginous hawks were capturing these animals at dusk or dawn, times

that ecologists refer to as "crepuscular," but I wanted
to rule out the possibility of nocturnal hunting. If
these hawks were indeed hunting at night, I reasoned, the most favorable time to catch them doing
so would be during a full moon.

The nest I decided to watch was along a desert
tract bordering some farmland. In one of the trees of
a long windrow dividing two fields was a ferruginous hawk nest that I had observed most of the
spring. These hawks were well into the nestling
stage, so my blind was situated about 100 yards to
the north in an open field. I knew of an active
Swainson's hawk territory less than a quarter mile
east, farther along the row of trees. I had discovered
a red-tailed hawk's territory directly behind me at
an abandoned farmstead to the north, and from time
to time a male northern harrier would also fly over
the northern edge of the ferruginous hawk territory,
coursing back and forth low over the sage and open
fields. As if these daytime raptors weren't enough,
during a couple of late evening observations a short-
eared owl made an appearance, beginning the night
shift. More than once I marveled at how busy that
square mile of real estate was, in terms of raptor activity. On occasion, I even jokingly mused over the
need of a raptor flight control tower.

It was after dark when I walked out across the
field to enter my blind for the nocturnal vigil. I heard
the haunting call of a great horned owl hooting to
the north, behind me. That accounted for yet another
raptor species in the neighborhood—one that I had
been unaware of. It was 10:30 p.m. and the moon
had not yet risen above the eastern mountains, although stars winked in the clear skies overhead.

Situating myself inside my blind as comfortably as I could, I glassed the nest tree with binoculars, silhouetting its shadowy form but nothing else. Around 11:00 p.m. the moon peeked above the mountains and began illuminating the landscape. Soon afterward, I was surprised to hear the brief but clear call of a meadowlark off in the distance. "Must be moonstruck," I thought. In the bright moonlight I could now see the dim form of the nest tree but still couldn't distinguish the forms of the resident hawks. Contenting myself with watching for any moving shadows about the nesting area, I detected something flying in a buoyant fashion over the fields just east of the blind. Glassing it with binoculars revealed a short-eared owl, very likely the one I had seen occasionally during late evening observations.

Things remained quiet and uneventful for the next hour. I couldn't quite decide whether sitting inside a blind in the middle of the night was more bizarre or more futile. But without doubt the moonlit scene outside was beautiful to behold.

Shortly after midnight, there was still no sign of hawk activity. Then, as I was scanning over the silvery landscape with my binoculars, I suddenly spotted something unusual on the ground between me and the nest tree. A small, shadowy figure, less than two feet tall, sat hunched over, periodically moving and bobbing a little. In the moonlight, I also could see what appeared to be feathers drifting off across the field, carried by the night breeze.

Puzzled and curious, I watched as this strange activity continued for nearly an hour. Finally, the movement ceased. Shortly, the mystery form seemed to expand as it lofted from the ground and flew seventy-five yards west to the top of a telephone pole that bordered the field. Was this one of my ferruginous hawks? No, but it was a large raptor-like bird and I was dying to know what it was. My question was answered almost immediately when I heard the mystery bird call out the resounding "whoo—whoooo—who—who—" of a great horned owl.

The surreal drama of that moonlit scene intrigued me. While the ferruginous hawks perched on their night roost in the nearby trees, I had watched both a short-eared owl and a great horned owl hunt the very same territorial space the hawks commanded during the daylight hours. Quite obviously the night shift had taken over.

By now it was after 1:00 a.m. and I was weary. I left the blind and retraced my steps to my V-W squareback, where I spent the rest of the night in the open back of the vehicle. I slept soundly until a robin's song awakened me at 5:25 a.m. I returned to the blind and, after putting in a morning stint observing hawks, I walked out into the field to see what the great horned owl had plucked and eaten during my vigil. Scattered about the spot were the wings, tail, and skimpy remains of a short-eared owl, probably the same one I'd seen hunting around my blind.

With this little moonlight drama in mind, I now had a better appreciation for the night stalker that seemed to continually haunt some of my ferruginous hawk nests. Unlike coyotes, I never actually witnessed great horned owls preying on hawks. Naturally, this sort of perfidy is most likely to occur under the cloak of darkness, with little chance of a human witness. But from time to time I did find some pretty incriminating circumstantial evidence of its occurrence.

The first case was perhaps the most impressive and conclusive.

It was late in my first year of study, and my partner and I were making the rounds at a number of ferruginous hawk nests, banding the young before they left the nest. As we walked in toward one of these nests at the fringe of a juniper thicket, we spotted an adult hawk perched on the ground at the base of the nest tree. It was the first time we'd seen this but we were new to the study of ferrugs and therefore didn't suspect anything unusual. However, as we drew near, the bird remained on the ground rather than taking flight and joining its mate in flying overhead, screaming at us. Now we suspected that something was wrong.

Cautiously we walked right up to the hawk, which opened its wings and mouth in a threatening display. It was apparently unable to fly, although we could see no obvious physical damage to the wings. I slipped my shirt off, tossed it over the hawk and secured the bird. Based on its size, we surmised this was the female. She lashed at us with her feet, but we easily restrained her. Rich and I gingerly gave the bird a brief inspection but still couldn't discern any obvious injuries. There were traces of blood on some of her chest and belly feathers, yet for all we knew, that could have been residue from recent prey. We carefully wrapped and tied my shirt around her. Rich, who was a falconer, fetched a falconer's hood and placed it on her head to cover her eyes, which helped calm her. She was obviously vulnerable in her incapacitated condition so we decided to take her back to Pocatello for veterinarian care.

During all this time the male hawk circled overhead vocalizing in protest. Having tended to the female hawk, we returned to the business at hand:
banding the nestlings. Working our way up the juniper to the nest, we discovered a dead nestling
along with its two live, healthy nest mates. The presence of fresh prey remains indicated that the male
was still delivering food to the nest. We tried to reconstruct what had likely transpired. It appeared that
some predator had made an attack at the nest, killing the nestling. Then the female must have inter-
vened, repelling the intruder before it could take the
young, but sustaining substantial injuries herself.
The culprit most certainly had to have been avian;
there was no physical damage to the nest structure
itself. We knew there was a great horned nest nearby
in the neighboring junipers, and its occupants immediately became our prime suspects.

In banding young hawks, it was our practice to
climb up to the nest, hand-grab one of the young
and bring it down to the base of the tree where it
could more easily be banded, measured, weighed
and the data recorded. Sometimes it was a bit risky,
especially when the nest contained older young, who
have an innate ability to employ their taloned feet
in defense. As I would cautiously peer over the edge
of the nest, these older nestlings would stand tall
and back away from me with their wings outspread
and beaks wide open in a menacing threat. Up to
this point, they inflicted only their piercing stare, but
it was a pretty convincing bluff. The next move was
mine. Smack in the middle of this stare-down, I
would very slowly reach a hand toward the closest
hawk and quickly latch onto its legs above its feet,

effectively disarming the bird. A brief flurry of wings would follow, as the nest mates defiantly lashed out at me with their feet while I lifted the flapping bird from the nest. Occasionally I would receive a minor scratch or puncture wound from handling these young hawks, but such occurrences were surprisingly rare.

Even though the adult hawks commonly swooped low over my head and screamed at me as I neared their nest, I was never struck by these diving attacks. In fact, my only serious injury from a ferruginous hawk was inflicted the day we found the injured female. After we hooded and bound her with my shirt, she lay quietly on her back in the shade. I was kneeling on the ground beside her, busily placing bands on her two nestlings. Engrossed in the process of my work, I shifted just enough that my leg lightly brushed her, unaware that I had touched her until she lashed out one of her feet and buried her talons in my inner thigh. It was lightning quick and caught me totally off guard. I dropped the bands and tried to release her grip from my thigh. Her large hind toe claw, or hallax, was buried deepest, and it took both of my hands just to pry loose the other three talons. Fortunately, I was able to summon Rich down from the nest to help me remove the hallax. Had I been alone on that day, one of our weather-bleached skeletons probably would still lie beneath that nest tree—I don't know how I would have gotten loose without doing a good deal of harm to myself and the hawk. I learned a great deal that day about the power and weaponry of an adult ferruginous hawk.

Being impaled by those talons posed far greater dangers to me than mere puncture wounds in proximity to the private parts of my anatomy. True, puncture wounds themselves always carry with them the risk of tetanus-causing pathogens and I'd need to obtain shots at the medical center back in Pocatello to counter that threat. But another danger worried me even more: contracting tularemia. This disease is closely associated with jackrabbits and is usually one of the major contributing factors to their population declines and rapid die-off. I was well aware of the fact that jackrabbits were a major food item for this hawk species and I was concerned about the microbes that surely occupied the talons that had just deeply pierced my body. Fortunately, a tetanus booster shot sufficed to keep me healthy and I never developed any symptoms of tularemia. But I did vow to pay more attention to my dealings with the talons of hawks after that experience.

The adult female died the following day at the veterinarian clinic after we returned to Pocatello. Examination of the bodies of the female and her dead nestling showed deep puncture wounds in the chest and shoulders of both birds. The pattern of those wounds suggested the zygodactylous (two forward, two rearward), symmetrical spread of the talons of a large owl. It was convincing circumstantial evidence—case closed, but no convictions.

This was not the only strong case for great horned owl predation at ferruginous hawk nests. Horned owls nested each year within a short distance of Penelope's nest. In all three years of my study, one of her nestlings mysteriously disappeared from her nest. I have little doubt that each year this was an unwilling, yet inevitable hawk sacrifice to the gods of the neighboring great horned owls.

Given the close protection provided to nestlings by the brooding female hawk, one may wonder how great horned owls could ever manage to sneak in and pluck a young hawk out of the nest. My observations of ferruginous hawk nesting behavior eventually suggested to me how this might happen.

During the first three weeks of the nestlings' life, they are small enough that the female is able to cover them during the cool night temperatures while brooding. After three weeks of age, however, young hawks are well feathered and they can huddle together for adequate warmth. They are so big by then that even the adult female cannot cover the large cluster of nestlings. I believe it is at this stage of the nesting season that the young hawks are more openly exposed to dangers such as marauding owls. Interestingly, most of the ferruginous hawk mortalities attributed to great horned owls during my study occurred to three to five-week old nestlings. As noted earlier concerning nocturnal raids by coyotes, I doubt that ferruginous hawks can wage a very extensive nighttime defense against marauding horned owls.

Owls have much larger eyes than hawks, with far more low-level light-sensitive cells called rods that help them see extremely well in the dark. Hawks, on the other hand, are active in the daytime when there is plenty of light and therefore have more sensory cells called cones, which operate best in bright light and provide good color vision. So owls have a distinct advantage over hawks for nocturnal vision.

I suspect it is during the curse of darkness that great horned owls become a greater bane to ferruginous hawks than even neighboring golden eagles. Although this eagle is a known predator of ferruginous hawks, literature accounts and my personal observations tend to suggest that the much larger golden eagle is generally less of a threat than great horned owls. I have watched numerous interactions between these two daytime raptors and always the hawk successfully drove the eagle from its territory. Similarly, other birds of prey researchers have reported seeing only minor conflicts between golden eagles and ferruginous hawks.

Golden eagles frequently ranged across a large sagebrush flat in one part of my study area, hunting low over the brush. I was there recording behavior at two neighboring ferruginous hawk nests, the ones later predated by coyotes. As I kept these nests under close observation during early spring of the third summer, I witnessed a dozen confrontations between the resident hawks and golden eagles.

By a mere quirk of luck I had found a measuring stick of sorts in these territories. A power line crossed both hawk territories and the distance intervals between the poles provided me a handy measure of the territorial limits granted the interloping eagles. For example, a golden eagle could perch undisturbed for hours on the fourth utility pole from one of the hawk nests yet, just as soon as the eagle advanced to the third pole, the resident ferruginous hawks responded by flying toward the eagle and began patrolling that end of their territory. If the eagle advanced toward the second pole, it was invariably attacked by one or both of the resident hawks. In most of the golden eagle confrontations, the ferruginous hawk flew directly to the intruder. Then, after the smaller, more agile ferrugs proved to the eagle that they had mastery of the air, the hawks fell in behind and gave chase.

One of the most intensive attacks I've seen on golden eagles developed in this area after the female ferruginous hawk dislodged an immature eagle from the third pole. Rather than leaving, the eagle went down to the ground between the second and third poles, well within hawk territory. A very hostile, cooperative attack ensued by the pair of ferrugs. The harried eagle seemed to throw its wings up in defense at each pass by its attackers. I couldn't tell if the hawks ever struck the eagle, but the vicious, alternating dives were highly reminiscent of the ferruginous hawk cooperative attack described earlier against the intruding coyote. Again, despite the much larger size of the golden eagle, the ferruginous hawks were able to mount a more effective defense against it than they could have against a nocturnal horned owl, due to their daylight-tuned eyesight.

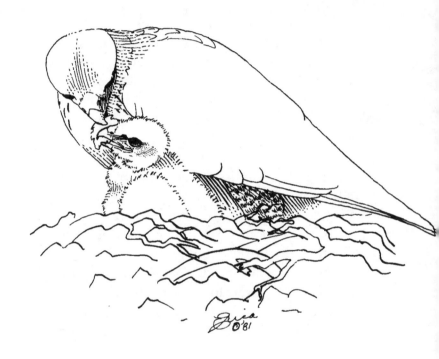

10

Moving In Close

A young ferruginous hawk's first confrontation with the environment begins early
within the egg. Although well protected from
the outside world by the egg's shell and inner mem-
branes, appropriate temperature and humidity are critical for sustaining that small life contained within. Since
this hawk is an early nester, during the month-long
incubation the eggs must be sheltered from the cold
winds and the blustery spring weather of April as well
as the hot, early summer days of May. As a rule, eggs
can better endure exposure to cool temperatures than
the desiccating effect of heat. In any case, diligent incubation and protection of the eggs is mandatory during the typically unpredictable spring weather in
ferruginous hawk country. Many days of close scrutiny at several nests over three years showed me that
seventy percent of the ferruginous hawk incubation
was done by the female, with the male covering the
eggs for periods of time when the female ate and took
breaks from her incubation duties.

Once hatched, the young chicks are suddenly thrust
into the precarious world, and still continue to rely on
the brooding adult female for shelter from the elements.
For the first four to five days, the female covers and
broods her chicks almost constantly, leaving them

exposed only briefly while she feeds them from the nest rim, or preens in a nearby juniper top. At this stage, a matter of a few hours exposure to morning or evening cold or to the heat of the day could prove fatal, as I learned the hard way from the "Camera Shy" episode described earlier.

The time arrived in my third summer of study when I needed to move in close to Penelope's nest for more detailed observations of nesting behavior. So on May 22, Tim and I assembled a blind at its initial location, fifty meters east of the hawk nest beneath a shading juniper. Good ol' "stay-at-home" Penelope did not even leave her nest as we carried in the blind parts and quickly assembled it. Instead, she hunkered low in the nest and merely watched our progress. We didn't want to disturb her further by checking the status of her eggs or young that day, but extrapolating back from a nest visit several days later, we learned that at that time she was brooding three two to three-day-old chicks.

It was also time for me to begin my efforts to document the ferrug's survival techniques for beating the heat of hot desert afternoons. Chuck Trost's original curiosity grew into a legitimate question as researchers in the Snake River canyon areas of southwestern Idaho reported that forty-one percent of golden eagle nestling mortality was due to heat prostration. Apparently, as the afternoon sun beat down upon three to six-week-old baby eagles in their cliff-side nests, they simply couldn't withstand the heat and many of them perished. On the other hand, my study showed that ferruginous hawks were not suffering mortality from heat stress at all, despite the fact that few of their nest trees provided shade of any kind to their eggs or young.

On the third and fourth days after placing the blind near Penelope's nest, I made a couple of morning observations, entering the blind before daylight. Viewing Penelope and her three nestlings through my spotting scope at forty-five-power provided intimate detail of their activity at the nest. Most of the time she sat covering her young and watching for the infrequent food deliveries from her mate. Incidentally, he never tarried at the nest but sat only briefly before departing within a few seconds of his food delivery, presumably to hunt for more food.

Already I could tell that prey selection at Penelope's nest reflected the bleak food availability following the jackrabbit population "crash" the previous year. For example, during those two mornings, the male delivered a small songbird, a kangaroo rat, a leopard lizard, and a ground squirrel—all dismally small prey for this, the largest hawk in North America, which thrives on rabbits. The energy demands on the male hawk to scramble for small prey was so much greater than the energy required to take a single, much larger jackrabbit that I wondered how successfully he would provide as the young grew larger and more demanding. This was definitely not the best of times for ferruginous hawks in the Wildcat Hills.

These first two days of observations showed that my presence in the territory was not hindering normal daily activity at Penelope's nest, so I prepared for my final, most daring and imposing study procedure. First, since the nestlings were now eleven or twelve days old, I wanted to try force-feeding my mini-mitters to the two larger young for the purpose of remotely recording their body temperatures from my blind. This use of radio-telemetry for recording physiological functions like body temperature, heart rate, or blood pressure is sometimes called biotelemetry. You must understand that despite all the high-tech gadgetry of today, I was pioneering the new technology of that era: time-lapse cameras and mini-mitters. My use of the mini-mitters, especially, was a bold new step, and I was more than a little apprehensive about its success.

If feeding the mini-mitters to the chicks went well, then Step Two was to set up another blind, even closer, so I could photograph in detail the nestlings' behavioral responses to heat stress, corresponding to the body temperature fluctuations I was recording via the mini-mitters. I was still gambling that Penelope would tolerate this up-close maneuver and allow me to place another, smaller blind nearer her nest.

For the first attempt at the biotelemetry experiment, I enlisted the help of my advisor, Chuck Trost. Since no one had ever tried this technique with young raptors, it was fraught with uncertainties. I was acting strictly on common sense and a basic understanding of hawk digestive anatomy. Truthfully, I really didn't know quite what to expect once I fed the transmitters to the baby hawks.

Late morning of the last day of May, Chuck and I visited Penelope's nest, where I climbed up and retrieved the larger two nestlings. After weighing and photographing them, we force-fed each a mini-mitter wrapped in a small morsel of kangaroo rat meat. I contemplated invoking the jingle "things go better with Coke" and recommending a shot of Coca-Cola for the nestlings but, given the gravity of the situation, I figured that this was no time for lame attempts at humor.

As it turned out, there was no cause for concern. The tiny one inch transmitters, each about the diameter of your pinkie finger, were easily swallowed by both nestlings. We returned the young hawks to their nest and retreated to my blind to see if we could pick up the transmitter signals. The moment of truth had arrived. We were stretching the limits of their range, but the beeping sounds they emitted were indeed audible from the blind. We began monitoring the number of beeps per minute and calculating the corresponding body temperatures for each nestling. I could easily convert the number of transmitter beeps to the bird's body temperature by using a chart I had developed earlier back in the lab, when I placed the transmitters in a water bath of known temperature and recorded their beep rate.

It was a bit crowded in the blind with the two of us but we were doing some cutting-edge science and didn't mind the inconvenience. We sat periodically listening to and counting the signal rate of the mini-mitters while, at the same time, observing and recording the behavior of the hawk family. To get readings of the ambient air temperature outside the blind, we employed the long-cabled temperature probe of another portable, battery-powered instrument called a telethermometer. It enabled us to easily correlate any fluctuations of the nestlings' body temperature with the air temperature around the nest.

It was a clear, sunny day and by mid-afternoon the ambient air temperature had climbed to eighty-five degrees, with only an occasional breeze.

Twice, for brief periods, Penelope "parasolled," or spread her wings, to cast shade on her young as she stood over them on the south edge of the nest. This behavior, which helps keep nestlings shaded and cool, has been recorded for several other bird species. Even though the afternoon temperatures were not extreme, already we were witnessing one of the ways the adult ferruginous hawk shelters her young from heat stress: providing shade not naturally available from the nest tree itself. Watching her added a whole new meaning to the expression "casting a long shadow."

We also got to watch a couple of prey deliveries by the adult male: both twelve-inch-long leopard lizards. Thereafter, Penelope periodically dissected portions of the prey and fed her nestlings. By four p.m., Chuck and I were feeling pretty confident about the performance of the transmitters, and the chicks had held down the mini-mitters without any apparent difficulties. To top things off, good ol' Penelope had shown off some of her parenting skills by feeding and caring for her chicks, and revealed how ferrugs play it cool in the hot afternoon sun. While the outside temperature had varied between seventy-five and eighty-five degrees Fahrenheit that afternoon, the baby hawks' body temperatures had fluctuated from one hundred degrees to nearly one-hundred-six degrees. Those body temperatures would be near lethal for humans, but birds' normal body temperatures are the highest of all vertebrate animals, typically around one-hundred-five degrees. The temperature data we collected became the first of several important survival clues about this desert hawk. I was eager to find out more.

Penelope briefly ushered Chuck and me out of the territory as we left the blind. Now the huge question was where would I find—or would I find—the mini-mitters when I returned to the nest? Due to commitments that drew us both back to Idaho State University in Pocatello, I had to wait three days before I could return to answer that critical question.

Back in Pocatello, I juggled academic matters at my graduate school office and enjoyed some family time on the home front, but the question of the fate of my mini-mitters continued to lurk in the back of my mind. I was more curious than concerned. I felt confident that no harm would come to the baby hawks. After all, their digestive system has a very acidic pH for dissolving food and is also designed to reject indigestible material as a part of a daily routine. But questions forced their way into my mind. What would their initial digestive process do to the exterior surface of the mini-mitters? I had taken the precaution of coating them with a thin layer of melted parafin for extra protection against the high acidity of the hawks digestive juices, so I really wasn't too concerned about damage to the transmitters themselves. My biggest uncertainty was the fate of the mini-mitters once they were cast up by the nestlings. What would become of them, then? I hoped that they would simply lie in the nest cup until I retrieved them. On my shoestring budget for the project, I was counting on being able to re-use these expensive devices several times during the course of the next month. I could hardly afford the $100 it would take to outfit myself with new transmitters after each use.

Finally, after mulling these thoughts over and over in my mind for a couple of days, early on the morning of June 3 Tim and I headed back down to Curlew Valley and the study area. We stopped and serviced time-lapse cameras at a couple of hawk nests, then motored on with increased anxiety and arrived at Penelope's nest just before noon.

11

Good Housekeeping
Ferruginous Hawk Style

When we entered Penelope's territory, Tim and I first placed a tube-like chicken wire frame on top of a low sand dune about twenty-two yards from the nest. This would later be covered with camouflaged burlap for my "close-up" blind and was about halfway between my existing blind and the nest. The small dune was elevated enough that I would have a reasonably good view into the open hawk nest from there. To keep it as low-profile and unobtrusive as possible, it was less that two feet tall and only about seven feet long. I would have to crawl into the blind from the back end and lie on my stomach to view and photograph the hawks through two small portals at the front.

By now Penelope had launched off her nest and was circling overhead, calling in protest at our intrusion. We were close to her nest so I turned on the receiver and listened hopefully for the familiar chirping of the mini-mitter signals. Nothing. Nothing but silence on both transmitter frequency channels. I quickly climbed the tree and inspected the contents of the nest. The three nestlings were in good condition, but where were my mini-mitters? I looked all over the nest and eliminated the possibility that the

transmitters were in the nest but non-functioning—
they were simply not there. My only consolation was
that the young hawks appeared very healthy and
that the mini-mitters had caused them no harm.

On the way down the nest tree I checked the pile
of sticks at its base, the remains of a woodrat nest.
These overgrown mice, also known as "packrats,"
are renowned for collecting shiny objects to orna-
ment their nest. I made sure the rodents had not
made a midnight raid on the hawk nest and pilfered
my mini-mitters. Now what? Where could they be?

Then it hit me. When I had checked the nest minutes before, not only were the transmitters gone, but
so were the castings from the nestlings. The scientific literature was beginning to report evidence that
some raptors remove prey remains from their nest
while young are still present. This "good housekeeping" behavior had not yet been described for the ferruginous hawk, but if there was ever a raptor that
might benefit from such a practice, this species was
it. For all species, the obvious benefit, or "adaptive
value," of nest cleaning would be basic nest hygiene
and the resulting reduction of nest parasites. But in
the case of the ferruginous hawk, especially ground
nesters, there would be the additional advantage of
reducing odors so there would be less scent to attract ground predators such as coyote, bobcat or badger.

I played this wild card. Maybe the transmitters
had been "cleaned" from the nest along with regurgitated pellets or prey remains. Receivers in hand,
Tim and I began to walk in wide concentric loops
around the nest tree, listening for any mini-mitter
signals. My assumption was that the adult hawks

picked up the transmitters with other nest debris, carried them out and dumped them away from the nest somewhere. It was my last remaining hope. As we began this last-gasp effort to find the transmitters, I wondered just how far from the nest they might be deposited—were we even on the right track?

We had walked through the sagebrush for only twenty minutes when, well over a 100 yards south of the nest, I began picking up a weak signal from one of my mini-mitters. For nearly an hour we worked back and forth in different directions following the strength of the signal until we finally triangulated to a point nearly 205 yards from the nest. There, on the ground on the grass amidst sagebrush, lay one of my mini-mitters. Elated, we quickly photographed the scene, retrieved the transmitter and beat a hasty retreat from the hawk territory in order to minimize our intrusion to Penelope and her mate. Even though we were a considerable distance from the nest by then, we were still within their territory and I wanted to give the hawks a reprieve from our presence. Momentarily savoring this small victory, we'd return later in the day to search for the other mini-mitter.

My excitement at discovering the dumped mini-mitter was two-fold. Not only did it look encouraging for the eventual retrieval of both transmitters, but I was quite by accident discovering some rather precise information about the "nest sanitation" behavior of the ferruginous hawk. This event is a good example of the serendipitous discoveries that sometimes accompany the daily grind of research focused in an entirely different direction. A little windfall sometimes rewards one for simply being out there, paying your dues and just *doing something*. As time went on, I would surely learn more nest-cleaning details.

Tim and I enjoyed a lunch of granola and jerky in the shade of some junipers a little less than a mile from Penelope's nest. Afterwards, while relaxing and giving the hawks a breather before our next search effort, I cleaned the air filter on my V-W squareback and amused myself by photographing male and female black widow spiders on their web in a nearby shrub. One of the things I loved about my hawk research in this broken desert country was the unending array of interesting animals and plants sprinkled across its landscape. Snakes, lizards, furry critters, colorful birds, and flowering plants constantly provided restful diversion during the occasional slack time in the day.

Around four p.m. a thunderstorm rolled across the valley, producing lots of thunder and some lightning but barely enough rain to settle the dust and momentarily cool the afternoon air. With the passing of the storm, Tim and I decided it was time to return to Penelope's territory and make another search for the remaining transmitter.

We began our grid-like search on the north side of the nest, opposite where we had found the other mini-mitter earlier in the day. After an hour and a half, we had worked our way all around the nest to the west and southward. We searched farther east and then cut another loop to the south farther out. We were 300 yards from the nest when we began picking up a faint signal. Triangulation took us quickly to a large grassy clearing where, much to my relief, we soon spotted the small red-and-yellow mini-mitter lying on the ground within six inches of a regurgitated hawk pellet. A conspicuous streak of "white-wash" or defecation next to the pellet and mini-mitter indicated the adult hawk had relieved itself of more than the pellets.

Piecing together the evidence, it seemed that one of the adult hawks had transported the mini-mitter and a pellet more than 335 yards from the nest and landed in this clearing with them. The close proximity of pellet, transmitter, and defecation suggested the hawk had landed on the ground to deposit the items—otherwise, it's unlikely the mini-mitter, pellet, and feces would have been together. As is a common practice with many raptors, the ferruginous hawk usually defecates just prior to taking flight, but seldom in flight. The adaptive value of dumping "nest debris" a considerable distance from an active hawk nest hit me again. Not only does this render a cleaner, more sanitary nest site but it leaves fewer smelly prey remains to attract the attention of passing predators.

After documenting our find, Tim and I went back by Penelope's nest, pacing off the distance from our mini-mitter dump point. There I slipped into the blind and Tim left the territory, playing a "numbers game" on Penelope. This procedure works pretty well with some wildlife species. When a reseacher wants to enter a blind during broad daylight with minimal disturbance to the subjects, two people go in, one comes out. In this case, Penelope saw intruders (Tim and me) enter her territory and subsequently she escorted the intruder (as Tim left by himself) out of her territory. Then she returned to her nest, seemingly satisfied that she had driven away the intruder. We assume the defending hawk cannot count or discern differences in people, and is therefore unaware that one intruder has remained hidden within the territory. Judging from Penelope's rather typical cessation of defense behavior and her return to "business as usual" back at the nest after Tim's departure, the numbers game works effectively with ferruginous hawks.

Back in my blind, I could see Penelope had quieted down immediately after Tim's departure and returned to her sentinel perch on a juniper next to the nest. The female's primary role throughout the nestling stage was that of sentinel and protector of the young. When she was not in the nest tree or on the nest itself she usually had several favorite nearby perches where she awaited food deliveries from the male. Then, after he brought prey to the nest, she typically proceeded to feed her young and herself.

As I continued observing the activity at Penelope's nest, I witnessed another nest sanitation behavior, this one performed by the nestlings. Standing up in the nest, the young hawks bowed their head, raised rear and wings, and clumsily backed to the nest edge where they defecated away from the nest. This innate behavior, also practiced by other bird species, squirts much of the feces outside the nest and has the practical advantage of reducing nest soiling. Because two or three young hawks occupy their nest for nearly fifty days, this behavior probably helps protect them from bacterial infection. I have even witnessed this behavior in tiny nestling hummingbirds. As I view this activity from time to time, I often wonder if humans were as innately fastidious about not soiling our immediate surroundings, would we produce less environmental pollution? Perhaps we, too, had that inclination at one time— but the excesses of our society probably expunged such concerns from our behavioral fabric.

For the remainder of my evening observation session in the blind, the chicks occupied themselves with preening, dozing, stretching their wings and occasionally playing with sticks in the nest. A little before eight p.m., Penelope returned to the nest and fed the remains of a horned lizard to one of the chicks. Near dusk, the nestlings dropped down out of sight as they began shuffling their way beneath Penelope's warm body.

By nine thirty p.m., even the meadowlarks had ceased their singing and relinquished the day. The moon was topping the eastern horizon as darkness settled in, so I left my spotting scope and tripod in the blind and carefully made my way out of the hawk territory toward my car. It was still warm enough that I had to maintain a constant vigil for rattlesnakes, which I encountered from time to time in this area. Tomorrow I would again feed the mini-mitters to the nestlings and record their body temperatures.

12

Surviving a Heat Wave

Before entering my large blind the next morning, I covered the front half of my ground blind frame with burlap so that Penelope might slowly become accustomed to its presence and accept it as a natural part of the landscape; I planned to gradually metamorphose it into my new hiding place. I then climbed up to the nest, and brought down one of the larger two nestlings for weighing. I dabbed a little bit of green food coloring on top of its head to distinguish it from the other two non-marked young who were different enough in size to distinguish. I fed the larger unmarked nestling, "White," a mini-mitter, accomplishing the task without the help of a meat morsel this time. The lack of meat didn't seem to matter to the chick; down the hatch went the transmitter. I only put the one transmitter out because I was working alone in the blind and elected to ease my tasks of observation and recording body temperature by monitoring a single chick. I retreated to the blind and began observing nest activities and monitoring the chick's body temperature. By now, it was nine a.m. and nearly eighty degrees outside the blind. With a coffee thermos full of cold water stashed at my side, I settled in with the hawks for a sweltering day in the desert sun.

By noon I had twice watched Penelope feed her nestlings; both times the prey was a kangaroo rat, obviously taken either the night before or around dawn this morning, since this rodent normally wouldn't be running around in full daylight. It was sunny and eighty-five degrees outside my blind. Thin clouds were beginning to subdue the sun and a light wind had picked up, relieving some of the heat stress on the hawks and me.

Already I had noticed new and interesting activities by the nestlings as the day heated up. They were exhibiting four subtle but distinctly different behaviors that I recognized as similar to those recorded for heat-stressed water birds in exposed nests on hot, sandy oceanic islands. First, the young hawks had clambered up onto the nest edge and then sat with their feet out in front of them. Next they gaped—that is, panted with their mouth open. Lastly, I noticed the nestlings sat on the windward side of the nest as they performed these behaviors, maximizing the cooling effect of the breeze that occasionally gusted to fifteen miles an hour. I knew that blood vessels in the mouth and the feet were being infused with warm blood from their body core and the air rushing over these surfaces was creating an evaporative cooling effect in the mouth and convection cooling of the feet. For the same reasons, a dog pants and people kick off their shoes on a hot day and dangle their feet in the breeze. Any one of these acts by themselves might not seem significant, but the combined effect no doubt helped relieve heat stress for these young hawks. As time went on, I would witness additional measures the hawks took to beat the heat of the desert afternoon.

While the young hawks employed these behaviors, I watched White's body temperature rise from one-hundred-two at ten a.m. to one-hundred-eight at noon, when the air temperature peaked at eighty-five degrees. As it slowly dropped through the afternoon to eighty degrees, the chick's body temperature lowered and remained around one-hundred-six, and it seemed to rest comfortably during this time.

At mid-day, Penelope's mate delivered a couple of lizards and another kangaroo rat to the nest. Penelope dissected these and fed them to the nestlings. The delivery of a kangaroo rat at this strange time of one-thirty in the afternoon hinted strongly that the male adult was food caching, or temporarily storing prey he had caught during the twilight hours of the day when this rodent is usually active. Food caching behavior is known in other raptors, too. It allows predators to maximize hunting at peak periods of prey activity and, later in the day, retrieve this excess food and deliver it to their hungry young at the nest when prey activity has diminished. The nocturnal kangaroo rat was no doubt snatched from the desert floor by Penelope's mate during the twilight hours of either dusk or dawn. Several times, Tim and I had seen male hawks actively hunting and feeding at these times.

The cloud cover was thin but complete by late afternoon and the outside temperature held at eighty degrees. The steady, light wind blowing through the junipers seemed to render the desert afternoon tolerable for both hawk and researcher. The nestlings were even able to find comfort enough to fall asleep on the breezy nest edge.

Although Penelope remained in fairly close proximity to her nest, sometimes I couldn't spot her from
my blind unless she vocalized, so I didn't always
know her exact whereabouts. Fortunately, two remote "hawk detectors" operated fairly constantly
around the nest site. One of these neighborhood
early warning systems was a pair of resident loggerhead shrikes that nested somewhere in the vi-
cinity and patrolled almost constantly. Their buzzy
alarm chatter kept me pretty well alerted to the location of either of the ferruginous hawks around the
blind. Interestingly, these masked birds, a little
smaller than a robin, are a true songbird yet they
live the lifestyle of a small hawk. Their upper beak
is hooked like a falcon, complete with the peculiar
notch, or "tomial tooth," which helps them dispatch
and eat their prey. Lacking the strong feet and talons of true raptors, however, shrikes often impale
their insect, mouse, or bird victims on thorns or
barbed wire to better anchor the prey while they tear
apart or "butcher" it. This mildly grizzly *modus op-
erandi* has given this bird the nickname "butcher
bird." In fact, the first part of its scientific name is
Lanius: Latin for "a butcher." It is the species name
of the loggerhead's larger cousin, the northern shrike
(*Lanius excubitor*), which hints at the "watch-dog"
quality of these birds. "Excubitor" in Latin means
"sentinel," so named by Linnaeus for its habit of
warning other animals of the approach of hawks.
So, true to their nature, the neighborhood shrikes
often warned me of the whereabouts or approach of
my hawks.

The other early hawk detector that often served
to alert me to the ferrugs' arrival at Penelope's nest

was a pair of western kingbirds that nested in a neighboring juniper. This bird, also robin-sized, is a flycatcher common to lower elevations of the West. Quite vociferous and excitable, these birds immediately become agitated and noisy at the sight of an approaching hawk. Between the kingbirds and the shrikes, I had fairly reliable informants who unwittingly kept me posted on the whereabouts and activity of the hawks around my blind.

At first it seemed to me that the smaller birds living next door to the hawks must live a precarious existence, under constant threat of attack by the hawks. However, if neighborhood predation occurred at all, it escaped my attention. At different ferruginous hawk nests there were even birds such as European starlings and house sparrows that nested and lived within the lower portions of the active hawk nest itself. These smaller tenants went busily about their regular routines, darting in and out of the lower nest structure with little apparent regard for the nearby larger, "landlords"—the hawks. So blatant was this benign association between hawk and small neighborhood birds, it suggested a sort of avian "amnesty" about the nest.

The benefit of this small-bird "Neighborhood Watch" set-up may have extended to the resident hawks, as well. The smaller birds sounded alarm calls at the approach of any and all threats, which could in turn serve to alert the resident ferruginous hawks to the encroachment of intruding, potentially dangerous predators such as coyotes, bobcats, and eagles. In return, the resident hawks' formidable defense against such predators extended protection to their more diminutive neighbors—perhaps a feathered feudal system of sorts.

By five p.m. that afternoon, things seemed to
have subsided to a restful lull at the nest. I gathered
my gear, left the blind and slowly made my way out
of hawk territory, delighting in the sweet stretching
of cramped back and leg muscles, and savoring my
second successful day of gathering body temperature data from Penelope's nestlings.

That evening Tim and I relaxed around our scant
desert camp, building a fire, and snacking on simple
vittles. In addition to Penelope's nest, I had a second hawk nest under surveillance a short distance
to the north, which necessitated this encampment
nearby in order to maintain a rigorous schedule of
pre-dawn and evening observations at the north nest
and midday body-temperature monitoring at
Penelope's nest. I needed these brief early-evening
respites, to re-hydrate my body after a hot afternoon
of baking inside my blind at Penelope's nest. Then
I'd switch to the blind at the north hawk nest for a
round of late evening watching. I also had a time-
lapse camera at the north nest that required regular
servicing to change batteries and film. Finally, at the
close of a long day, somewhere on the fringe of the
Wildcat Hills, we'd spread our sleeping bags out on
the desert sand beneath the stars, secretly hoping
the local rattlesnakes wouldn't find the warmth of
our bedding too much to their liking. On more than
one occasion during the middle of the night, I was
startled by a kangaroo rat bouncing off my chest as
I lay huddled in my sleeping bag. No doubt these
nocturnal rodents were both plentiful and active
throughout the night in this sandy, desert grass and
shrub terrain. Who knows how many of their kick-
boxing scampers I slept through, but perhaps these

bouncy rodents helped divert the snakes from our cozy beds.

It wasn't just the threat of passing rattlesnakes or periodic communal dances by kangaroo rats that sometimes postponed sleep on those nights in the Wildcat Hills. Strangely, we often suffered from the pestilence of mosquitoes: insects you'd expect nearer to water, but not in the middle of dry, dusty desert reaches. Although unlikely assailants, even during the more comfortable parts of the day in my blinds, I found them pesky. Scattered throughout my field notes are blood splotches here and there on the pages with a little "Bonzai!!" inscribed next to them—mute testimony to the demise of another tormentor. Apparently, these tiny, winged Draculas drifted up on the winds from the wetlands of the Salt Lake basin south of us.

I didn't mind the inconveniences or, in some cases, even the potential danger posed by some of these desert creatures. To me, they represented close encounters of the naturalist's kind, merely part of the adventure of studying this desert hawk. When I probed the floor of my blinds for rattlesnakes in the predawn darkness, chased scorpions out later in the day and constantly checked for stowaway black widow spiders, I respected their place in the landscape. I didn't even begrudge the mosquitoes. They lived there; I was the sojourner. I never tired of being awakened to the nocturnal serenade of a distant coyote. The yips and howls always stirred an echoing response from somewhere deep within me. It was as though the piercing call harkened me back to the old days of the wild West. As it trailed off, I wondered if the nearby ferruginous hawks also were listening. Several times I awakened suddenly in the middle of the night, not knowing what had aroused me but feeling an eerie sense of uneasiness. I'd raise up in my sleeping bag, scan the nighttime landscape around me and strain for telltale silhouettes or sounds. Suddenly a flare would burst among the stars of the southern sky and I would realize it was activity related to night maneuvers out of Hill Air Force Base far to the south.

One night while encamped among the rocks and junipers of the Wildcat Hills, I was just preparing to slip into my sleeping bag when a gigantic dark figure sailed overhead, silently at first. Then the tremendous roar of jet engines shook the ground beneath me. It was a low-flying jet bomber on some ground-hugging nocturnal practice run. Invariably, while I was alone at night in those remote desert hills, sudden flashes in the sky, or ominous swooping shadows overhead would conjure up unnerving thoughts of UFO's and alien life forms. In truth, the frequent thoughts of venomous snakes, scorpions, and spiders were less disturbing to me than those occasional unexpected bursts of humanoid activity from the airbase.

I rolled out of my sleeping bag in the dark of predawn the next morning, slipped on my boots and heavy shirt and made my way through the brush and junipers to the north nest. As I slowly entered the territory, crawling over some large boulders, I heard the plaintive call of an adult ferruginous hawk in the direction of the nest. From its sound, the bird was in flight. Before entering the blind I went through my brief ritual of opening its door and probing around the blind's sandy floor with my camera tripod, checking for any rattlesnakes that might have sought shelter therein since my last visit. Fortunately, that never happened, but I took no chances. The mere thought of crawling into one of my blinds and finding myself face to face with a startled rattlesnake was enough to keep me wary.

It was five-fifteen a.m. when I settled into the blind with my gear. As daylight gradually resolved the landscape in front of me I began to make out the shadowy forms of the three young hawks huddled low within the nest. The increasing light, however, still did not enable me to locate the adult hawks. After another half-hour of observation, the female still had not returned to the nest site and I grew concerned that perhaps my early morning entry had disrupted normal activity here at this nest. I decided to vacate the territory and let things calm down. Maybe I could return a little later with Tim and play the numbers game and get back into the blind for a brief session of observation.

Leaving the blind and winding my way through the junipers and boulders, I soon discovered that the female hawk had been perched on a juniper nearly a hundred yards north of the nest all the time. She called and flew overhead, joined by her mate, and they escorted me out of the territory.

As I made my way among the junipers back to camp, I enjoyed the sights and the sounds of sunrise in these desert hills. An adult and two juvenile great horned owls peeked at me through the lacy foliage of a large juniper. Their presence bode restless nights for the neighboring hawks. In fact, Tim pointed out to me later, maybe it was the nearby presence of these owls that had prompted the hawks' unusual perching locations that morning. In any case, I was glad to turn my attention to the lighter antics and benign presence of the plain titmouse, rock wrens, and mourning doves, who also made this juniper community their home.

After another simple excuse for breakfast, Tim and I returned to the north nest and changed film in the time-lapse camera. I entered the blind. Then Tim distracted the adults with his departure. We had noticed the male hawk at this nest liked to perch on a lone juniper on a rocky promontory north of the nest. An owlwatch, I wondered?

It was shortly after seven a.m. and I was once again secretly ensconced inside my blind, ready to pry into the private nesting life of this little-known desert hawk. I never ceased to feel the thrill of this potential learning experience. Piece by piece, I was gathering tiny bits of information that I hoped would eventually form a whole—a complete picture of life at the nest of the ferruginous hawk. I hoped that picture would disclose the age-old secrets of their survival in the harsh environment beneath the relentless desert sun. Often, at the beginning of these sessions, I prayed that I would not merely look through the eyes of an observer but that I might have the wisdom to see with some insight and understanding what it was I was watching. The wealth of hawk activity that unfolded before me, engrained by successful generations of the bird's strife and struggles with its environment, had to be filtered through my frail senses and interpreted by my meager understanding. Obviously, the challenge was staggering and I never felt completely up to the task.

But I labored on, as much through the pure fascination of sharing the wild intimacy of this hawk's life, as for any hope of unveiling much of its meaning. I didn't know it then, but I think I was living out the advice written twenty years later by Edward O. Wilson when he said:

> Love the organisms for themselves first, then strain for general explanations, and with good fortune, discoveries will follow. If they don't, the love and the pleasure will have been enough. [*]

Toward the end of my three-year study, word had gotten out about the work Rich Howard and I had been doing, and about the sizable ferruginous hawk population we had uncovered throughout our study area. Consequently, other researchers had become interested in conducting raptor studies along the Idaho-Utah border. One such person, who will remain nameless, started a project at the north end of my study area, making extensive observations from blinds on the hunting activity of ferruginous hawks. Meeting him one day in the field, I cordially asked how things were going for him and his study. His reply was that he didn't particularly enjoy his project and could hardly wait to "get out of this hell-hole!" I was first shocked by his response, then offended, and finally felt more than a little sorry for him. Although my days were typically long and exhausting, I can't remember a single one when I wasn't excited about the mere prospect of adding one new little piece of information to the picture I was slowly

[*] Edward O. Wilson. 1994. Naturalist. Warner Books, New York, NY. p. 191.

assembling on the nesting life of the ferruginous hawk. In fact, by my second summer of study, I had abandoned the use of an alarm clock to awaken me early in the day—often an hour before daylight. I anticipated each field day with such passion for discovery that it didn't matter that I had been up until midnight the night before, transcribing audio-taped field notes onto paper. For me, from beginning to end, this was all a labor of love.

Things remained quiet and inactive about the nest for nearly an hour after I returned to the blind. I wondered about the success of Tim's efforts right about then. After leaving me at this blind, he was going to take my biotelemetry receiver to Penelope's nest to see if he could locate and retrieve the mini-mitter I had fed to a nestling for body temperature monitoring the day before. As I had done so many times already this summer, I once again felt most grateful for Tim's company. Not just for his most pleasant and enjoyable companionship, but also for his willing and able assistance, which allowed me to accomplish so much more than I ever could have done alone.

The three young hawks were now up and about, defecating out over the nest edge, preening, and nibbling gently at each other's head and beak. Nearly three weeks of age, their downy covering was beginning to erupt in a patchwork of dark pinfeathers along their wings. The medium sized nestling suddenly jerked its head up and seemed intent on watching something passing overhead and to the west. The jabbering of a magpie from that direction suggested the likely object of the young hawk's attention.

The nestlings soon settled back down low into the nest and appeared to sleep. Then, a few minutes later, they suddenly were aroused by the arrival of the adult male with a prey item in his left foot. Through the spotting scope I had a detailed look at this fine-looking bird. Like Penelope's mate, this male was mostly white on its belly and flanks, but had thin pin-striping down its neck and upper breast. His feet were noticeably smaller than those of the larger females. This was a trait that soon became evident even among nestlings as they neared fledgling age. For nearly five minutes the male sat on the nest edge. This event was also recorded on the time-lapse film. It was one of the longest sessions I witnessed during the entire nestling stage for a male to remain at a nest following a prey delivery. Typically, such prey deliveries lasted less than five to fifteen seconds.

Soon after the male departed, the medium-sized youngster began pecking at the prey item in a futile attempt to feed itself. Its two nest mates seemed content to sleep. Less than ten minutes after her mate's departure, the female returned to the nest carrying a twenty-four inch stick in her beak. She stood on the nest, looking around for a few seconds, before dropping it on the nest edge. Transporting nest material to the nest was a periodic activity that continued well into the nestling stage, and may have served to refurbish and add cleanliness to the progressively tattered nest as the young hawks grew in size and activity. These little nest additions may also cover some remains of errant defecation on the nest edge, adding a touch of nest sanitation as well.

The adult female's arrival at the nest seemed to perk up the nestlings, who now were all pecking at the prey item, a kangaroo rat. The adult female looked conspicuously larger than her mate, who had appeared just minutes before at that same spot. The larger nestling began making head-down gagging motions and soon cast a small pellet. Another nestling picked up the kangaroo rat in its beak and unsuccessfully tried to swallow it whole. The female gingerly took the prey from her nestling and, pinning it down in front of her with both feet, began to dissect and feed it to her young. A couple of the young still persisted in trying to peck at the prey at their mother's feet. She continued to butcher and feed them tidbits of the rodent, until it was mostly gone. The female then stepped away from what was left while two of the young continued to peck at prey remains within the nest. As the female departed, she pecked at something at the nest edge and then turned and flew out of sight. It happened quickly, but I suspected she took some debris out of the nest with her—nest sanitation behavior, perhaps, or "house cleaning".

Within the next ten minutes, the male made two rather quick deliveries of prey to the nest. On the first arrival he sat for nearly four minutes, and for more than two minutes the second time; both were extremely long nest visits and both deliveries were kangaroo rats. One of the kangaroo rats was pretty small and, much to my amazement, one of the larger nestlings succeeded in swallowing it whole. I wondered if, during a low in the rabbit cycle such as we were experiencing, the preponderance of small prey delivered to the nest hastened the onset of or otherwise enhanced self-feeding by the young hawks. They seemed much better at simply swallowing small-sized prey items than they were at dissecting larger ones.

The morning had remained overcast and cool, and mosquitoes became voracious in the blind. I became more and more curious about Tim's success in retrieving the mini-mitter from Penelope's territory.

By mid-morning it began to sprinkle outside, so I concluded my observation session at the north nest and walked back to camp. Tim was there. I was relieved to hear he had had no difficulty in locating and retrieving the mini-mitter. He had found it on a small, bare, low mound 125 yards south of Penelope's nest. It was lying next to a pellet. Both were wet, suggesting they had been freshly cast and recently removed from the nest; roughly twenty-four hours after we fed the transmitter to the nestling. There was also the tell-tale white streak of defecation near the dumped items, again suggesting the adult hawk had landed on the ground with its payload and then defecated before departing.

Tim and I planned to return to Pocatello that day, but before leaving the Wildcat Hills we walked into Penelope's territory and finished covering the frame on the ground blind twenty-two yards from the nest with camouflaged burlap. When I returned to the study area the next week I would conduct my observations and monitoring of the mini-mitters from that site. That would be a landmark event of monumental significance to me. It represented the culmination of nearly three years of study, and would be my closest ever look into the nest life of a ferruginous hawk. I was eager to return.

The passage of any week in the life of a ferruginous hawk can bring deadly events. When I returned to Penelope's nest, I found mute evidence of this. Knowing that nest failures due to weather, predators, or human vandalism were common occurrences in a hawk's life, I was relieved at Penelope's greeting as I entered her territory after my absence. Mistakenly, I was once again pleased at her reassuring presence and the usual signs that things were as they should be. I suspected nothing was wrong until I climbed the nest tree and peered into the nest. The young hawks had grown in size but had diminished in number. One of the two smaller nestlings had disappeared. I could still see traces of green food coloring on top of the head of one of the remaining chicks, so I knew the missing member wasn't "Green." There was no other evidence of foul play at the nest.

Fratricide, or the killing and eating of one's siblings, is a well-known phenomenon among a variety of predatory birds, including several raptor species. It seems that, in the face of food shortage and probable starvation for all, the larger, more aggressive nestlings will sometimes kill a weaker, smaller sibling and then consume its carcass. Perhaps it's a rather grim hedge against starvation and the loss of all the siblings—a sacrifice at the expense of the smallest and weakest nestmate, a grisly activity that carries survival value for the current nesting investment.

Though well documented for some raptor species, to my knowledge there had been no evidence of fratricide at ferruginous hawk nests. My own observations, most of which occurred during food shortages accompanying a jackrabbit population crash, found no other evidence of fratricide or cannibalism at this species' nests other than the unexplained disappearance of a nestling now and then. Therefore, I attributed the loss of Penelope's nestling to predation by nearby great horned owls. It seemed to be an annual event at her nest: when her nestlings were in that critical age of three to four weeks, too large and bulky for Penelope to brood at night, one would disappear. They were vulnerable to quick nocturnal attacks by great horned owls. Still, I sometimes wondered about these disappearing nestlings.

I fed the mini-mitters to the two remaining nestlings and returned them to their nest. They were getting large enough to be aggressive in their defense as I handled them. But once they were released onto the ground or back up into their nest, they exhibited the more typical non-aggressive "hiding" behavior, where they dropped low and remained motionless and passive. At this stage in their life they probably could avoid danger as much by hiding as fighting or trying to flee.

Before climbing down out of the nest tree, I strung the telethermometer cable from the nest edge, down the tree trunk, and to my ground blind where, concurrent with the chicks' body temperatures, I could take readings of the environmental temperature at the nest site. Placing my gear in the new ground blind, I left the area. Before monitoring the activity at Penelope's nest, I needed to visit the north nest and service the time-lapse camera. I was working solo this trip, and sorely missed Tim's assistance. Now everything I did took longer.

Returning to the ground blind for my first observation session from this ultra close vantage-point,
I crawled into the tube-like burlap blind situated
atop the small sand dune close to Penelope's nest,
and immediately began recording body temperatures of the two young hawks. Already, at nine-forty-
five a.m., the outside or ambient temperature was
nearly eighty-five degrees. I had a superb view of
the nest and its occupants from my new blind on
the sand dune. I was also close enough to get an adequate view through my camera's four-hundred-
fifty mm telephoto lens for recording hawk behavior
on film.

The two nestlings remained fairly quiet until the
adult male swooped over my ground blind and
landed at the nest with a kangaroo rat. I could hear
the rush of his wings as he departed back over my
blind. The soft sounds of the hawk passing immediately overhead were a stirring reminder of how close
I now was to their nest. "Let the good times roll!" I
thought, smiling in anticipation. The smaller, unmarked nestling, "White," began what was to become a common food-begging vocalization or
"eeep" call. I seldom heard this sound from the larger
nest mate, but the "eeep" call was a fairly constant
ranting from White until he was either satiated by
food or fell asleep. I didn't know if it had been going on during earlier observations and I was too far
away to hear it, or if it was something just now showing up in the nestling behavior.

During this observation session, I also heard considerably more food begging from Penelope as well.
Her hunger call was a strident, harsh vocalization
she would variously repeat depending upon her

mood. When I had first heard this call from one of my blinds a year earlier, it reminded me of a male mountain quail's call, and in the beginning I didn't even associate it with the hawks. It took me a while to pin it down as the adult female ferruginous hawk's hunger call. The call would intensify whenever the female sighted her mate nearby, especially if he approached the nest with food. In fact, if Penelope were out of my sight, often her sudden outcry of food begging would alert me to the imminent arrival of her mate with prey.

Soon, Penelope arrived at the nest with a lizard, which White quickly grabbed and eagerly gobbled down. By now it was almost noon and the day remained sunny and calm. Ambient temperatures at the nest had risen to ninety degrees but the young hawks had settled down and were quiet.

At one-fifteen p.m. the temperature at the nest was ninety-five degrees and the nestlings were beginning to thermoregulate by gaping and panting while they sat on the nest edge with their feet out in front of them. The male brought another lizard to the nest and one of the young hawks quickly consumed it.

Increasing cloud cover and a light breeze lowered temperatures at the nest to near ninety degrees by mid-afternoon. This brought enough relief to the nestlings that they both quietly slept at the nest edge. Thunderstorms began to build to the southwest and by four p.m. intermittent thunder rumbled in the distance. The cloud cover continued to lower the nest temperature to eighty-six degrees, and the young hawks responded to the reprieve in the weather by getting up and preening. Despite the moderating weather and temperature conditions, I was beginning to feel the toll of a long, hot afternoon of lying in the sand in my burlap blind, so I took a break and left the territory to seek some shade and sustenance of my own. But just before leaving the blind, I lost White's mini-mitter signal inexplicably—for some reason I could not pick up any signal at all from that transmitter!

A refreshing breeze stirred in the shade of the juniper I was sitting under. That and copious swigs of water with a few handfuls of homemade "Gorp" worked wonders to revive me from my sun-baked afternoon in the ground blind. The day had started out as one of the hottest yet, and the potential for heat stress on the young hawks was great. Ambient temperatures had ranged from eighty-five to ninety-six degrees before the mid-afternoon build-up of thunderstorms with their accompanying clouds had dropped the temperature by ten degrees. The hawks' body temperatures had varied from one-hundred-five to one-hundred-nine degrees and closely followed the up-and-down trend of the surrounding temperatures. During the hottest time, the nestlings employed their behavioral tricks of perching on the nest edge with their feet out front into the breeze and panting to keep cool.

By six p.m. the storms had passed, the winds calmed and the late afternoon temperatures soared again. Curious about the heat stress on the young hawks, I returned to the ground blind and took a set of temperature readings from the hawk nest. Air temperature was ninety-nine degrees at the nest. Still no signal from White's mini-mitter. Green's mini-mitter reading indicated a body temperature of one-hundred-nine degrees. I decided to visit the nest and take White's temperature manually, since its mini-mitter had failed. I found both chicks with their heads and forebodies in the scant shade available at the nest when I climbed up to take White's temperature. White's cloacal temperature, the same as a rectal temperature for humans, taken with the use of the telethermometer probe at the nest edge, also read one-hundred-eight degrees. It was reassuring to me to find that my two temperature recording devices were in agreement on the body temperatures of the two nestlings.

In fact, I found the agreement of the body temperatures especially intriguing in light of the conventional wisdom floating about at that time. The debate more or less held that if researchers directly handled a wild animal such as I had just done to manually take the cloacal temperature of the young hawk, that their presence and handling of the subject would likely inflict such nervous trauma on it that that alone could alter its body temperature and lead to erroneous data. That was why I had designed my research for measuring body temperature with the mini-mitters; I could record body temperature changes remotely from my blind without imposing my presence and causing any nervous response in the birds that might muddle the data. So, although this was but a solitary comparison, at least this one instance of agreement of data from the two measuring techniques didn't place much stock in the concerns about "hands-on" trauma. That debate aside, reckoning that I had imposed myself on these hawks long enough for one day, I left the area and the hawks to their evening activities.

As the month of June wore on, I continued monitoring temperatures at Penelope's nest and photographing the thermoregulatory behavior the hawks
employed to survive the grueling heat of the hot
desert afternoons. The growing nestlings added a
few new variations to their behavioral repertoire of
survival tricks as time went on. Increased feather
growth and its insulating qualities forced the nestlings to ruffle their plumage during heat stress to
create openings to the underlying skin through
which body heat could more easily escape and
breezes could more readily cool. Likewise, they began using a wing-drooping posture by holding the
wings open and away from the body, to provide an
open-air breezeway around the body.

In mid-June temperatures within my study area
were especially hot, with some mid-afternoon air
temperatures around Penelope's nest ranging between one-hundred and one-hundred-nine degrees.
Even today, a quarter of a century later, a few of those
days in the summer of 1974 still hold the record high
temperatures for parts of southern Idaho—I understand why, and remember them well! During those
torrid times, the young hawks were extremely restless and obviously heat stressed. They restlessly
shifted around the nest seeking shade, and sometimes would lie in the shade of the perched adult, or
crowd beneath a nest mate in an apparent effort to
exploit the slightest bit of shade available. Panting,
wing-drooping and ruffling their feathers, these
sorry young hawks sometimes voiced their extreme
discomfort with a stress vocalization that was a series of "chit-chit-chit "calls. This array of activity persisted throughout the heat of the afternoon until

cloud cover, wind, or evening brought a reprieve from the blazing inferno. Then, the young hawks would quiet down and doze peacefully. Later, in the relative cool of the evening, the nestlings seemed invigorated, moving about, preening, flapping their wings, and alertly watching the small world around them.

Incidentally, after the third feeding of transmitters to the nestlings, I was always able to recover the mini-mitters directly from the nest—I didn't have to scour the territory with my receiver. It seemed that nest-cleaning behavior by the adults waned after the young were about three weeks of age.

13

Beating the Heat: Adaptations to a Hot Environment

By the end of June, Penelope's nestlings were large and healthy and nearly ready to fledge from the nest. Day after day, from inside my sweltering ground blind, I had witnessed their struggle to survive the searing elements of their open desert nest. I had documented the ferruginous hawk's fascinating array of anatomical, physiological, and behavioral adaptations to a hot environment. Here are some of them.

One anatomical adaptation is the species' extensive gape. In other words, the corner of the ferrug's mouth extends to, or beyond, the mid-point of its eye, unlike the mouths of other closely related broad-winged hawks. In fact, that feature alone enables identification of a ferruginous hawk even when only the side of its head is visible. This wider gape results in a large orifice laced with a profusion of tiny blood vessels near its surface. Of course, multitudes of tiny, unseen capillaries are connected to those blood vessels. So what do this unusually wide gape, extensive mouth surface, and profusion of blood vessels have to do with staying cool in a hot environment? Or, in other words, how does it benefit a heat-stressed hawk?

Some biologists maintain that the ferrug's wide gape is an adaptation to feeding on jackrabbits. Since I've yet to see a ferruginous hawk swallow a jackrabbit, and I've noted many rabbit leg bones picked clean of meat around ferruginous hawk nests, I'm not too taken with that idea. In my observation, larger prey, such as rabbits, are dissected and eaten in morsels. If it relates in any way to feeding, perhaps it is an adaptation for quickly gobbling kangaroo rats while the hawks are optimizing their brief crepuscular hunting of these rodents. Although that may be handy for the hawks, I doubt that it has exerted very much selective pressure over the eons.

Rather, I believe that the large, heavily vascularized (numerous blood vessels) gape of the ferruginous hawk is advantageous in lowering its core body temperature by evaporative cooling. As the bird pants and wets its mouth, it dissipates heat carried to the oral cavity by all those blood vessels. This is a common mechanism, known to be used by numerous animals, including many birds. While it may not be the wide gape's only useful adaptation, I believe it to be the important one, and my behavioral observations strongly support that conclusion.

Beyond basic anatomy (that is, the form and structure of this hawk), my measurements of body temperatures of ferruginous hawk nestlings pointed up a more purely physiological adaptation to a hot environment. (Physiology relates to the inner workings or dynamics of an animal's body systems. For example, you and I, as humans, maintain a rather high, constant body temperature around 98.6°F. As I pointed out earlier, birds have an even higher body temperature, typically well over one-hundred degrees. There is grave danger to us if our body temperature rises or falls much above or below the norm, and the same is true for other vertebrate animals, including birds.)

In winter outdoor sports we hear concerns about hypothermia (when body temperature drops below normal levels). In the heat of the desert, I found that young ferruginous hawks tolerated the equally dangerous hyperthermia, or elevation of body temperature above normal levels.

We all can recall our mother's or a medical doctor's grave concerns over an extended fever because it could do irreparable damage to living tissue, and therefore, our body. For you and me, even a brief period of one-hundred-five degrees body temperature would be life-threatening. Yet on more than one occasion, I measured midday fluctuations of nestling hawk body temperatures from one-hundred-one to one-hundred-ten degrees. This represents a remarkable toleration of hyperthermia. The ability to simply endure it seems to be unique to young ferruginous hawks. Such a heat load would likely kill the nestlings of other raptor species. For instance, heat often has been implicated in mortality at golden eagle nests, although I don't know how many eaglet deaths have been documented with actual body temperatures.

Two years after my study of ferruginous hawks, one of my students and I used these same minimitters to measure body temperature of a single young golden eagle near Nampa, Idaho. Four weekly measurements of the eaglet's body temperature at weeks five through eight remained around one-hundred-one degrees, although these measurements were never taken during ambient temperatures over eighty-five degrees and therefore the eagle was not likely to have been heat-stressed during that time.

If an animal can tolerate such extensive hyper-thermia, it will begin to lose heat, thereby lowering its temperature. That's because heat moves from a point of higher temperature to that of lower. So a hot body will lose heat to cooler air or surroundings. Once you (or a hawk) are hotter than the surrounding air, your body temperature will fall. The trick to cheating fate here is being able to tolerate the heat for a short while. Not many animals can handle that scorching demand, but the ferruginous hawk can and does include that in its survival bag of tricks.

Much less subtle than the ferrug's anatomical and physiological adaptations for surviving heat stress were the hawks' behaviors while seeking relief from the heat. Shade was a practically non-existent but magical presence at the nest. This fundamental cool-ing agent is known and used throughout the animal kingdom, but not many of the nests in my study area bore much foliage for potential shade. The impor-tance of shade to young hawks was highlighted in some of my time-lapse photos. Speeding up the ac-tivity captured on film, they reminded me of a jerky, old silent movie of "shade tag" being played in the nest by the downy chicks. The frames of film had been exposed or "taken" at two- to three-minute in-tervals, so imagine the resulting film shown at regu-lar speed. At first you notice dark shade patches jerkily moving about the nest as the day rapidly progresses on film. Then, as you look again at the same images, you notice the obvious and slightly delayed movement of the downy chicks right along with the shade. It almost appears that the shade is playing some sort of "I got you last" game with the young hawks, but the chicks quickly and persistently catch back up to the shifting shadows and dive into their comforting coolness.

The surprising thing about the ferruginous hawk chicks' instinctive shade-seeking behavior was that it began when they were barely five days old—just as soon as they could move and become heat stressed. It may all start as an instinctive movement toward the parent figure. The adult female typically spent lots of time perched at the nest and she often provided enough shadow that the nestlings would lay resting and sleeping in her shade. Time-lapse photos and direct observation revealed that the female sometimes deliberately spread her wings and tail to cast shade over her young in a "parasol" or sun-shade effect. This behavior also has been reported by other ferruginous hawk researchers in Utah and Washington State. Not only did the nestlings seek the shade provided by the female and tree foliage, but when heat stressed they also moved into the shadow provided by standing nest mates, to the point of scooting beneath them with their heads protruding out between their siblings' legs.

The young hawks began to move out of the nest cup onto the edge of the nest, usually into the wind, once they were over ten days of age. By that time, they were more mobile and less apt to be brooded by the female. As mentioned earlier, by orienting into the wind, the chicks gained even more benefit from its cooling effect by raising their feet out in front of them. I measured nestling foot temperatures several times and found that typically the feet were cooler than the body temperature but hotter than the surrounding air temperature, which allowed the hawks to lose body heat to the cooler air by simple convection.

Panting, wing-drooping, and ruffling of the feathers are all known means of cooling a bird's body. They were practiced regularly by older nestlings, as well as adults. On a couple of occasions I observed Penelope wing-drooping and panting during hot afternoons, thereby also benefiting from this heat-losing behavior.

One of the more subtle tricks the nestlings used to prevent overheating in the nest was related to their activity level. The young hawks' daily activity periods were critically linked to the sun. The hotter it got, the slower they moved. Before the sun's rays struck the nest in the cool of the early morning, the nestlings remained huddled together in the center, either sleeping or resting quietly. As the air temperature increased after sunrise, the nestlings would sit up or stand around the nest, often engaging in preening, exercising, or social interactions with each other. However, from mid-morning to early evening things changed. That was the most stressful time for the young birds. Much of that scorched time of day was spent trying to beat the heat with their repertoire of thermoregulatory behaviors: nest-edge perching, wind-orientation, wing-drooping, panting, feet-out-front perching, and ruffling body feathers for ventilation. But whenever possible they would fitfully rest, since the less muscular activity, the less body heat produced and the better off they were.

Marshalling their entire bag of tricks, the young ferrugs endured the discomfort of another day in the sun. As temperatures subsided after sunset, new life seemed to energize them. They stood up and once again moved busily about the nest, seeming to bask in the cool of the evening. Finally, near nightfall, the chicks ceased all activity and again settled low into the nest cup beneath the desert stars. They had survived another sun-baked day. Now, only an errant swirl of warm air might whisper across their nest, recalling what they had endured that day and foreboding of what would surely come again on the morrow.

More than once, as I stood in the juniper shadows and bid my hawks goodnight, I shared their sense of deliverance from the parched afternoon and marveled at their resiliency and the triumph of their survival. All was well, I would think. And then the distant hoot of a great horned owl would filter through the junipers and, with a sudden chill, I was reminded just how tenuous survival can be in the desert.

Since I was completely thwarted in my efforts to study ground nesting ferruginous hawks, I often pondered their plight in the afternoon sun. How did they fare compared to tree nesters? What mitigating or exacerbating factors prevailed in their situation? I can only point out three obvious conclusions. First, all the adaptations I identified in tree-nesting hawks could certainly work to alleviate heat stress in ground nesters, as well. Second, at most ground nests, shade is usually non-existent at the nest itself. However, once the nestlings become fairly mobile, at about three to four weeks of age, they are able to move to the shade of nearby shrubs or rocks.

A friend once showed me a photo of a young ferruginous hawk from a ground nest huddled in the shaded entrance of a nearby badger burrow. So shade is probably inherently more restricted at a ground nest itself, but more readily accessible all around the nest to mobile young, long before they are able to fly. Third, since most ground nests are near the crown of bluffs or escarpments, during the hottest part of the afternoon the updrafts common at these locations will constantly move air over the nest. In any event, the incidence of ground-nesting ferruginous hawks is a testament to their apparent survivability.

14

On Wings Like Eagles

My first discovery of a ferruginous hawk territory in the early days of my study remains forever etched in memory because a magnificent flash of white wings heralded the occasion. In the remote reaches of sagebrush and junipers in Curlew Valley, I had just pulled my vehicle to a dusty stop to inspect a suspicious-looking object perched atop an isolated juniper in the distance. Neophyte that I was, I could barely recognize ferruginous hawk habitat.

Nonetheless, I was on the search for ferrugs in what I thought might be a suitable desert area. About the time I rolled down the window and reached for my binoculars, the object took to the air with a spectacular flare of white wings. It reminded me of a gigantic white butterfly or a huge albino bat, but with a quick, shallow wing beat. Then I heard a shrill, whispy call as the bird banked and winged my direction before it circled higher and higher overhead. I gawked in awe at my first look at a territorial ferruginous hawk protesting my invasion of its secluded land.

For many birds, flight is more than a unique means of conveyance from one place to another. (I say unique because, if you think about it, precious few species on Planet Earth can hurl themselves through the air and sustain that trajectory in continued flight. Mastering this means of movement places birds, bats, and insects in a very select group.) But back to my main point: flight often becomes more than mere locomotion. Flight endows birds with an aerial pen with which to scrawl ornate messages in the sky. It can be, in a word, communication! What sort of ethereal language did I find among the ferruginous hawks? Interestingly, their wings fairly shouted in their silent grace.

In 1892, Charles Bendire, an Army captain turned ornithologist who was stationed for a time near Lewiston, Idaho, offered one of the first descriptions of the flight of the ferruginous hawk. In his words, "Its flight is rather slow, but graceful nevertheless; it seems to take life easy and be but seldom in a hurry."

I think Bendire's impression of this hawk's seemingly nonchalant flight is really a reflection of its power and mastery in the air. I soon noticed that even during spring storms, when blustery winds buffet the entire landscape, this hawk wings its way with apparent ease. Catching the wrath of the wind, it folds and flits its wings like a huge barn swallow, then with grace and agility exploits the energy of the ambient turbulence to its own bidding.

I was in for two surprises as I continued to record the flight capabilities of the ferruginous hawk. As much as the first surprise was disappointing, the other was simply unexpected.

One type of flight I had eagerly anticipated documenting for this hawk just never materialized: aerial courtship choreography. Many raptors have aerial courtship displays that are breathtaking. Falcons cliff-race, harriers sky-dance, and I fully expected great things from this spectacular hawk.

Most birds of prey species engage in courtship flights. When I started my study of ferruginous hawks, however, only the behaviors of those species with the most outstanding flights were well known; flights, for instance, such as the northern harrier's dramatic undulating or "roller-coaster" maneuvers punctuated with spectacular dives near the female or nest. Occasionally, the male red-tailed hawk soars above the female with legs dangling, or with prey suspended from his talons. In most cases this "sky dancing" is a bit of a feathered laser show —brief but definitely worth watching. I could hardly wait to see what sort of aerobatics ferruginous hawks might display in their amorous flights.

That turned out to be my first big surprise about this hawk. For three years, early each spring I patrolled the study area and greeted the ferruginous hawks as they arrived at their nesting territories from the south. Never did I see anything that faintly resembled a courtship flight. To this day, ferrugs are the only species of buteo in the northern United States for which a courtship flight has never been described.

But don't hasten to brand this hawk as an inept lover or a lackluster Romeo. In human terms, the male of the species is probably the female's ideal: Its style is to really "build" on its relationship with the opposite sex. Apparently male ferruginous hawks forge a strong social bond with their mate by investing extensive time in nest construction and courtship feeding. As mentioned earlier, this lengthy period of cooperative nest-building results in one of the largest of raptor nests, as well as a strong pair bond.

Truth be known, unless they culminate in copulation the "undulating," "sky-dancing" and diving flights performed by raptors around their territories and nests often can be ascribed to non-courtship functions such as advertisement, territorial marking or patrolling, and defense of territory. What had over the years been viewed as raptor "courtship" flights have more recently been proven to serve these other functions also.

It is not only the gathering of nesting material and the cooperative shaping of it into a nest that serves as important courtship behavior for the ferruginous hawk. Another activity also plays a prominent role in forming and maintaining the pair bond: courtship feeding.

During courtship feeding the male hawk delivers food to the female, and this often culminates in copulation. Most of these food transfers occur at the nest site. Despite this "home delivery," the female hawk invariably flies away from the nest with her food and lands on the ground before eating it. Perhaps this is related to the "nest sanitation" behavior I documented with my mini-mitters.

Courtship feeding benefits hawks in many ways. First of all, recall that hawks are some of the most fierce, aggressive, and independent of the predators. To make courting even more hazardous, female raptors are larger than males. Both sexes tend to be quite solitary. Obviously, a need arises each spring for males and females to get together in rather chummy and intimate ways. How do they overcome these obstacles?

One fairly disarming and universal gesture of friendship and togetherness is the offering of free food. And so it is in the raptor world. The proffered food is quite timely for the female. In addition to providing a means of uniting the pair and strengthening and maintaining the pair bond, it certainly gives the female the extra energy required to bring her into reproductive fitness for egg production. Courtship feeding may further serve to anchor the female to the nest site. Even if copulation doesn't always follow, courtship feeding clearly signals reduced aggression in the male and acceptance and gradual readiness for mating in the female. Certainly, early courtship feeding by the male sets in motion the necessary practice of bringing food to the incubating female and, more importantly, to the nestlings later.

My disappointment at not finding some razzle-dazzle courtship flight by the ferruginous hawk was abated somewhat by the other surprising discovery. Contrary to the current field guide descriptions of the day, the species did indeed practice the unusual flight known as hovering. This helicopter-type maneuver is typically the province of smaller, more agile birds of open areas, where the activity serves as sort of an aerial "perch" enabling the bird to search the terrain beneath for moving prey. Hovering is commonly seen in bluebirds, kingfishers, and a smaller raptor, the American kestrel. But I often observed male ferruginous hawks hovering, especially on windy days with gusts of at least fifteen mph. Interestingly, I never saw this flight practiced by the females. Perhaps they are just too large and bulky to pull it off.

Hovering is a common practice of the ferruginous hawks' smaller cousin, the rough-legged hawk, which lives in the open treeless tundra at northern latitudes. Given the open country inhabited by both these species, and the male's vital role as provider for the entire family, hovering may be an important addition to the male's hunting repertoire. Perhaps it's one more advantage of the male's smaller size.

I noticed other very conspicuous flights performed at times by ferruginous hawks. Eventually, through careful documentation of when and under what circumstances these flights occurred, their purpose and likely function became clearer to me.

As I expected, this hawk could soar with the best. Soaring in easy circles overhead is both a hunting strategy for large, broad-winged hawks, as well as a handy way to patrol large territories. Keen-eyed hawks can survey large expanses from that height and remain in a commanding position for quick descents for defense or prey capture. Some buteo or broad-winged raptors are known to ride wind thermals more than 10,000 feet high. On hot days, such a high soaring altitude may even serve them as a means of cooling off.

Generally, the male ferruginous hawks did most of the soaring, while patrolling their territory. I often saw them hunting several hundred feet high, nearly a mile from the nest. But make no mistake, the graceful circles penned by their wings ascribed subtle territorial boundaries to watchful neighbors. Many times I saw male hawks choreograph their soar into a rather pointed message to intruding raptors. They were veiled threats in the form of a deliberate escort through the ferrug's territory. The aggressive element of this escort was blunted markedly by the relative position of the ferruginous hawk, which typically soared below the intruder, yet definitely was following the interloper across the territory. The defused aggression of staying below the interloper likely renders their escort less threatening because of the poor potential for attack from the inferior position.

Although this "follow-soar" occasionally erupted into an attack or chase, more commonly it only involved escorting intruders from the territory. I saw male hawks follow-soaring with sharp-shinned, Cooper's, rough-legged, and Swainson's hawks. On occasion, usually out near the fringes of their territories, the ferrugs even escorted golden eagles in this manner.

Occasionally, immediately after the male had escorted another raptor species out of the area, he would dive steeply, plummeting from high overhead down onto the nest or a nearby perch within his territory. In such cases, these steep dives seemed to serve as a territorial advertisement signal or perhaps a warning to intruders, and reassurance to his mate—an exclamation mark of sorts.

More than a dozen times I watched male hawks perform a flashy flight never before described for this species. In fact, on three of those occasions, the flight preceded the steep dives I just described. The conspicuous features of this aerial behavior were deep wing beats with banking and twisting in a very buoyant flight, somewhat reminiscent of the bouncy flight of short-eared owls. In all instances, the resident male ferruginous hawk performed this deep-winged, bouncy flight in the presence of intruding raptors. I think it was an aerial signal announcing the displaying bird's territorial rights and serving as a warning to interlopers. It seemed more intense when the intruders were other ferruginous hawks, a little less animated in the presence of closely related hawks such as the Swainson's and rough-legged hawks, and least animated when they escorted more distantly related hawks such as northern harriers and golden eagles.

In retrospect, I think the flight I most commonly associate with the ferruginous hawk is the one that impressed me on the first day I beheld a territorial hawk soaring overhead. That fluttery flight, which I eventually named the "flutter-glide," became a common sight and seemed to precede many of the hawk's territorial advertisement and patrol behaviors.

All the forms of visual sky-talk I witnessed in this bird's flight were no doubt highlighted by its large, white-colored body, which flashed across the open country. What better way to etch its signature across its domain?

At best, I probably missed far more than I saw in this hawk's flight behavior. Such is the challenge and the "work in progress" nature of behavioral studies. What at first appears to be the fairly obvious purpose of an animal's activity may later prove to serve other functions. This is particularly true of courtship or mating behavior.

It is a slow process, trying to figure out why wild animals perform certain behaviors, even with such mundane activities as flight. Time and again you wish you could simply ask them why they just did something, like psychologists do with their human subjects. Regrettably, the animal language barrier forces us instead to make painstaking, repeated observations of that same behavior, noting in excruciating detail the context or setting in which it occurred. Then, mentally dissecting the circumstances piece by piece, we sometimes can identify enough common elements to figure out the cause and reason for that action—if we're lucky.

An example of deciphering the complexity and multiple functions of seemingly ordinary mating behavior is my occasional observation of ferruginous hawk copulation that occurred well into the incubation stage, long after it would have served any function in fertilizing the female's eggs. Dr. David H. Ellis, a golden eagle researcher in Montana, also had noticed this behavior in that species. So, if mating didn't serve the usual function of fertilization, what was its purpose?

Comparing notes, David and I concluded that these non-fertilization bouts likely served variously as territorial displays, a means of maintaining pair bonds, helping to time reproductive readiness or, in some cases, as displacement behavior—that nervous expression of agitation in conflict situations.

In this multiple-use economy of behavior, perhaps I did see shades of ferrug courtship flight after all. What's to stop the flashy aspects of the territorial flights from also impressing the female hawk? By a show of flexing their muscles in many of these aerial maneuvers, perhaps the male ferrugs were showing off to their mate—courting, if you please—as well as defending territory. As my friend R. Wayne Nelson suggests, some courtship behavior may not always be "in your face" razzle-dazzle, but more subtle, woven into the fabric of other flights. In any case, the ferrug's language of flight is rich and varied and still somewhat open to interpretation.

15

From a Far Valley

Early each spring I patrolled the large valleys of my study area in search of the first arriving ferruginous hawks and often found only uninhabited terrain. My hawks were apparently still in some far valley. Often only the distant flapping movement of an occasional eagle or raven enlivened the landscape. Yet even the seemingly deserted days of early spring in those lonely reaches sometimes struck a fanciful grandeur all their own. I vividly recall one blustery afternoon when I hiked to the top of a bluff-like promontory and surveyed the far reaches for the slightest trace of white that might herald the presence of the first ferruginous hawk. As the wind buffeted me, I beheld an incredible "stampede" across the valley floor below.

It looked like a sea of gray-bodied animals in a wild race for their lives, sweeping northeast across the valley. Momentary flashes of the "thundering herds" of Zane Grey days sprang to my mind—for in truth, at first glance I believed I was watching an honest-to-goodness stampede! Quickly it dawned on me that instead of sheep, cattle, or mule deer in synchronous motion, it was a sea of bobbing, rolling tumbleweeds extending more than a mile. The wind provided the roar, and the distant rolling mass of Russian thistles provided the movement. It was an unforgettable sight. I felt like a lone ghost rider commanding the stampede from my lofty desert pinnacle.

On another spring afternoon of a different year I was inundated by a massive stampede of a different sort—this time it was butterflies. I was in the lower Curlew Valley along the west side of the Wildcat Hills. I stood entranced by the flow of butterflies swirling around me like the turbulence of a shallow, aerial stream. Neck deep in butterflies, as far as I could see in the distance the desert floor shimmered with their flight. Although I didn't know butterflies well in those days, I'm fairly certain they were painted ladies, which are one of the few migratory butterflies other than monarchs.

On certain years, when conditions are just right in Mexico and the Southwest, the painted ladies swarm across the western United States in a mighty and conspicuous movement. As they fluttered across the valley floor that day, they gave the illusion of a landscape in motion. I still recall how the sight of them made my spirit flutter as sprightly as did they.

Usually, it wasn't until the last of February or early March that ferruginous hawks appeared, suddenly, like white sentinels again perched along the sagebrush-and-juniper fringes of the valleys. I often wondered from whence they had returned—from which far valley? Where had Idaho's ferruginous hawks spent their winter? I hoped to answer these questions with the results of my banding efforts.

With help from friends I banded nearly 150 ferruginous hawk nestlings during the three years of my study. Although I had also contemplated the possibilities of trapping and banding adults, their propensity for nest abandonment discouraged me from attempting that. I didn't want to mess with their susceptibility and behavioral sensitivities any more than I absolutely had to. Besides, any information from the banding returns of the young hawks would give me pretty good clues about the wintering activities of all Idaho's ferrugs.

Before we continue, you must understand a well-known premise of bird banding. That is, to learn much from this activity is a painfully slow process with notoriously meager results. The rule of thumb assumed by bird-banders is you're lucky if you receive information back from one bird out of every 100 you band. Of course, you understand that banded birds don't fly around spouting off their band numbers to any and all interested parties. Instead, the shy and elusive creatures must be taken into the hand again, dead or alive, in order to gather much subsequent information. Therein lies another problem.

There are precious few bird-banders throughout the West available to live-capture a bird that has already been banded. This does happen, but not very often. The more likely way for a banded bird to come into someone's hands is if the bird is found dead. Regrettably, sick and dying birds commonly seek the shelter of cover before their demise and are much less visible for discovery in such hidden places. Add to that the likelihood that any sick, dying, or dead bird is prone to be eaten by ever-present predators or scavengers, and you can understand the infinitesimally small chances of recovering banded birds.

On those rare occasions that a dead bird is found by a person, it is seldom inspected closely enough to notice a banded leg. Consequently, most banded birds are easily overlooked, making it necessary to band lots of birds if one hopes to glean much information from such efforts. Garnering much banding data simply requires a measure of luck.

Despite the dismally low rate of information return from bird banding, it still remains useful, for how else can we unravel some aspects of avian life history? The kinds of information provided by the recovery of a banded bird might include when, where, why, or how the bird was encountered the second time. That sort of data then can offer further clues to a host of other unknowns like longevity; distance traveled from the place of banding; and faithfulness to nesting sites, wintering areas and mates; as well as causes of death. It is this *potential* wealth of information that continues to spur numerous researchers to engage in this time-consuming and laborious business.

To improve the chances of gathering information on my banded hawks, I fastened colored plastic wing tags on most of the nestlings. This technique had been tested and found successful in other raptor studies, so I obtained permission from wildlife authorities to use them in my ferrug research. I wrapped small plastic streamers around the front edge of the wing, or patagium, and then riveted them together between the flight feathers of the trailing edge. Armortite or Saflag brands of plastic cloth obtained from tent manufacturers worked well. These materials were soft, yet quite durable, and came in a variety of colors. The tags were far more conspicuous than the metal leg band alone, and since they could be seen and reported by observers without actual capture and handling of the birds, I hoped that sightings of these color-marked hawks might give me additional clues to their late summer movements and winter migration.

Humorously, one of my first "sighting reports" came surreptitiously from one of Chuck Trost's old sidekicks in Germany where, according to his fictitious report, a couple of my color-marked ferruginous hawks were seen frequenting a downtown Bavarian pub. With righteous indignation I totally discounted that claim solely on the grounds that my hawks hailed from staunch Mormon country and grew hale and hearty under my Protestant surveillance. It seemed hardly possible that those young hawks could have gone bad so quickly. On the other hand, a rigorous religious environment has been known to drive the occasional adolescent to rebellion!

Jokes aside, I did get some interesting feedback from my banded and color-marked hawks.

I often wondered how many people actually saw one of my marked hawks and never reported it. Such sightings have a way of lingering solely in the memory of the observer and never going beyond. Most people simply don't know where to report their sightings or, if they do have a clue, never get around to doing it. Although I did receive three or four sighting reports, most of my information came from bands found on dead hawks.

Earlier in this book I mentioned the case of one of the two "abductees" Rich and I rescued when our early camera placement attempts went awry. That particular young hawk perished in northern Mexico. Others were reported from Texas, southern California, New Mexico, and one way-faring young bird wound up in southern North Dakota—obviously a male, or it would have stopped and asked directions! Others died before they even made it out of southern Idaho or northern Utah.

Virtually all these reports occurred during the first months after hawks fledged from their nests— the time of highest mortality for most young birds. Leaving their home territory poses many hazards, especially while they are learning the gritty business of hunting on their own. At that same time, they must survive inherent dangers lurking along the terrain of migration. At best, migration is a risky business that few survive.

Even before my young hawks were old enough to band, I occasionally observed mortality among them. Eight young hawks perished before leaving their nests, apparently from natural predation, all cases strongly implicating great horned owls. At least nine other nestlings were taken by coyotes. I found an additional young hawk that apparently starved after falling from its nest, perhaps after being blown out by the wind. The "nest-edge-perching" behavior that young ferruginous hawks employ to keep cool on hot afternoons renders them vulnerable to sudden whimsical wind gusts from passing thunderstorms. I found at least two other nestlings on the ground after storms and returned them to their nest. I was a bit surprised that the one "grounded" fatality was not fed by its parents, even while at the base of the nest tree. Perhaps it had been provisioned but not sufficiently, for there were two healthy siblings still in the nest. Oddly, neither adult was present at the nest during our visit that day. Since it was during the lean times following a jackrabbit decline, it's possible that the scarcity of prey forced both adults to hunt away from the nest.

In contrast to this natural mortality that snuffed out young hawks at nest sites, most of my band returns suggested death came from human-related causes. For example, at least three hawks were shot and two were struck by automobiles. Another perished in a tar pit created by highway construction waste. The cause of death for three other young banded hawks was simply reported as "unknown," giving little clue to their demise. Remember that according to the expected mortality of young birds, roughly two-thirds of my 150 banded ferrugs were not likely to survive their first year. Also as expected, very few bands would be recovered—as evidenced by the few above mentioned cases. Oh, to know the fate of all the others!

As those occasional mortality reports slowly filtered in, they raised nagging questions that hounded me for many subsequent years. What about those few hawks that did survive that grim first year? They would likely live on for some time still wearing my bands. Would I ever, eventually, get any reports from them? And if so, how long must I wait before their eventual deaths might yield such recoveries?

I mentioned earlier that in this bird banding business sometimes plain old luck can play a role. Such was the case with the only report I have yet received from one of my older hawks. It came by way of a phone call to my office several years ago.

Dan Gossett, a raptor biology student at Boise State University, was on the other end of that surprise conversation. He had been trapping adult ferruginous hawks in portions of my old study area in Curlew Valley as part of his graduate project studying the "morphometrics" of the species. (Basically, he was measuring some of the body size differences between male and female hawks.) In 1991, an adult male hawk he captured at a nest near Stone, Idaho, wore a band I had placed on it in 1974! Dan recaptured the same hawk at that nest the next year. Thus, eighteen long years after I banded all those young ferruginous hawks, I finally learned my first bit of longevity information from one of the survivors.

This gives an idea of the excruciatingly slow process, yet the abiding triumph that accompanies such banding successes—by a stroke of good fortune. I was doubly thrilled about this whole incident because that chance recovery of information came from a bird that was healthy and alive at the time of its discovery! It probably survived several more years.

Okay, so what was the take-home message delivered by this eighteen-year-old hawk? Nearly two decades after I had held this young male in my hands and banded it as a nestling, he still lived and nested less than a mile from his natal nest tree. In all likelihood, he had occupied that same territory throughout most of those intervening years. Dan Gossett's trapping intervention documented what we had long suspected: young ferruginous hawks return to their place of birth for nesting and likely live to be twenty years of age or older.

Coincidentally, about the same time as Dan's encounter with my banded ferruginous hawk in

Curlew Valley, I was seeing similar evidence in another ferruginous hawk population. I had banded these young during the early 1970s in a juniper stretch along the north end of the Idaho National Engineering Laboratory (now INEEL) near Arco. After I found a number of nesting ferruginous hawks there, it became sort of an unofficial extension of my Curlew Valley study. Its remoteness from the rest of my study area, however, presented such logistical problems for travel that I restricted my efforts to merely banding young hawks at the end of the nesting season.

In two different years during the early 1990s, while conducting Breeding Bird Surveys with some of my students along that same stretch of the INEEL, I spotted a banded adult ferruginous hawk. I knew that few people besides Tim Craig and me had ever banded ferruginous hawks in that part of the state. So, in all likelihood, that adult was fifteen to twenty years old and packing one of the bands that either Tim or I had placed on it long years before.

After seeing that banded adult on the INEEL, the urge festered within me to muster an all-out campaign to revisit all of my old ferruginous hawk territories and look for banded individuals. The plan was to then trap those birds and verify their history as revealed by the bands they wore. To my great frustration, the press of life, and work responsibility always prevented me from acting on that dream. Way led onto way—and finally I knew I'd never return. Since it has now been more than twenty-five years since I banded all those hawks, it is doubtful that many, if any, of them are still alive.

One reason this recent longevity information from my banded ferruginous hawks did not totally surprise me was because of a clue offered by a remarkable piece of similar information in the old, old scientific literature. Given the time and manner in which that record occurred, it is even more astounding.

Apparently, during the winter of 1917, someone attached a leather collar to the neck of a ferruginous hawk at Clayton, New Mexico. Fastened to it were a bell and a name plate bearing the return address and date (January 7, 1917). Some 20 years later, presumably during the spring of 1937, that hawk was found dead at Strongfield, Saskatchewan, Canada. The bird was reported to have wintered in the Clayton, New Mexico, area during 1918 and 1919 and to have nested in the same tree at Strongfield for the four or five years prior to its death. This unusual means of marking the hawk occurred before more standard banding techniques had been established. Yet, in its crude but ingenious way, it contributed one of the few pieces of longevity information known today about the ferruginous hawk.

In conclusion, what do we now know about the year-round movements of Idaho's ferruginous hawks? Both old and new banding studies have given us a pretty good picture of their annual habits. For example, they seldom occupy their nesting territories throughout the year. Typically, food availability wanes around these beleaguered sites by late summer, and resident hawks drift off to greener, more productive hunting ranges. There are occasional exceptions, especially during high jackrabbit years when the abundance of this prey may allow hawks to remain close to their territories throughout the winter.

Tim and Erica Craig noticed this during the peak jackrabbit year of 1981-82 in southeastern Idaho near the INEEL. That winter the burgeoning jackrabbit numbers not only held the resident ferruginous hawks near their territories but also attracted large numbers of golden and bald eagles. Such explosive numbers of rabbits not only eased the chore of hunting but also greatly increased the availability of roadkills provided along the highways criss-crossing the Arco desert.

However, this rampant proliferation of jackrabbits occurs only every eight to ten years, if at all. Sometimes a variety of environmental factors operate to dampen these population upswings. Thus, the Idaho hawks I studied commonly drifted away from their nesting territories in late July and ended up miles away in some of the higher mountain valleys like Gray's Lake, Henry's Lake or Island Park. Nestled against the west edge of the barrier of the Rocky Mountains, these hawks subsisted on the plentiful supply of Richardson's ground squirrels until rodent hibernation and favorable fall winds prompted their southward migration in early October. With this changing of the seasons, they would wing their way into the more favorable winter clime of some far valley. For many, it was their final and fatal journey—but for a precious few, Idaho would again be a summer home.

16

Side Shows and Serendipity

Perhaps one of the greatest lessons that my hawk study taught me as a naturalist had little to do with ferruginous hawks. Rather, it was the simple realization that my daily field work regularly brought me face-to-face with unexpected, sometimes startling but often fascinating, little sideshows in nature. Most of these "mini-adventures" had little bearing on my real purpose for being there. But the key to these serendipitous surprises was the fact of my simply being out there! Wandering about this remote back-country as I did from day to day occasionally landed me smack in the middle of intriguing discoveries.

Lizard Safaris and Baby hawks

While I worked alone in my blind during the early morning observation sessions, Tim remained back at our camp and enjoyed the luxury of sleeping a little later into the morning. By the time the rising sun had warmed the surrounding shrub-land and rocky outcrops, Tim's terra firma bed had usually grown sufficiently uncomfortable and he would get up and eat a simple breakfast. Then, he'd occupy himself by reading and taking short hikes to explore the interesting flora and fauna of the area. There was also the daily task of feeding and caring for the injured short-eared owl that he was rehabilitating after it had sustained a wing injury. Tim was responsible for the owl's care back on the I.S.U. campus, and since "owl babysitters" were hard to come by, Tim's field excursions necessitated bringing the owl along as a travel companion. The stoic owl sat on a padded perch, tethered safely by falconry jesses. The gimpy bird handled this traveling quite well and it soon became our regular field mascot. While parked outside the Snowville Café, the sight of the owl perched in the rear of my V-W Squareback occasionally attracted a momentary crowd of onlookers.

Fresh food, meat of some kind, was a daily requirement of this owl. For the most part procuring this daily fare was not a great chore because we easily hand-captured kangaroo rats along the desert roads in our headlights as we traveled along after sundown. However, Tim being a life-long hunter, soon discovered another, equally entertaining way of acquiring owl food. He found my hand-made blowgun—just a five-foot length of electrical conduit, which I had used to capture lizards in some of my past herpetological studies. Corks embedded with a flat-headed nail were the ammo, and the velocity of the corks, powered by a strong puff of breath was sufficient to stun even the foot-long lizards of northern Utah. By varying the power with which you blew on the cork inside the blowgun, one could also vary the speed and resulting impact of the projectile so that it would strike a stunning blow commensurate with the size of the critter you were hunting without killing it; assuming that you hit your target —which took considerable practice. Of course, gauging the power with which you blew on the blowgun, and its resulting velocity on the cork also took practice. If you blew too hard, the impact of the projectile killed the lizard, especially smaller ones. On the other hand if you blew too softly you lost speed, power, and accuracy, and simply startled the lizard into a quick retreat to cover. Consequently, the constant teaser was: to blow harder for greater velocity and accuracy—a temptation tending toward fatalities.

Living among the rocks of the Wildcat Hills where we often camped were not only several species of desert snakes but also a fair number of large lizards. I had often seen them delivered as hawk food at Penelope's nest, especially during the third summer when jackrabbits were scarce. The two larger lizard species, each over a foot in length, were the long-nosed leopard Lizard (*Gambelia wislizenii*) and the western whiptail (*Cnemidophorus tigris*). When the rising sun heated the boulders these lizards crept out and prominently sunned themselves on the rocks. Not only were they inviting morsels for hawks, but also tempting targets for Tim and the blowgun. Often while awaiting my return from my early morning observations at the hawk nests, Tim succumbed to the ancient genetic predisposition to hunt and spent the morning stalking and blow-gunning lizards among the rocks. In the beginning Tim's accuracy improved but his breath calibration lagged behind so the occasional lizard fatality served as owl food. In time, however, Tim's enthusiasm and deadly aim outstripped even his owl's appetite and he devised a clever little scientific experiment in which to employ the extra dead lizards.

His idea was simple. Tim began feeding the left-over lizards to the "runts" in neighboring Swainson's hawk nests. He reasoned, that by comparing their survival with similar young of other nests, he might see if his supplemental feedings increased the number that survived to successfully fledge from those experimental nests. Often, especially in time of food shortages, the smallest chick in a hawk nest does not survive. Unfortunately, Tim soon realized that his sample size of experimentally fed young was way too small, and he also lacked other unsupplemented nests as "controls" with which to compare survival rates. In the end, the bounty from his "lizard safaris" served only to feed his gimpy owl and several runt-sized, hungry baby Swainson's hawks! But who knows, perhaps two or three young Swainson's hawks survived that summer solely because of the extra food offerings from "Uncle" Tim.

Horny Toads and Love in the Sun

One of my first serendipitous discoveries was hardly an event at all and could so easily have gone unnoticed. In fact, apparently it had gone completely unnoticed since time immemorial, for what I witnessed had never been reported before and remained significant enough that I eventually published a scientific note on it.

It was a sunny, late May day of 1972 in early afternoon and I had just visited a ferrug nest in lower Black Pine Valley. Discovering downy young hawks in the nest, I was making a quick exit from the nest tree back through the sagebrush to my distant car. Always on the lookout for rattlesnakes, I was picking my way through the brush when some movement on the ground in front of me caught my eye. In a small bare patch of ground were two horned lizards or "horny toads". Stopping, and giving them a quick scrutiny, at first I thought that they were fighting. The smaller of the two lizards was on top of the other, and they appeared to be scuffling. Then I concluded that "horny toads" was an appropriate nick-name for these particular individuals as it dawned on me that they were, indeed, in the act of mating. As with humans, copulation among most wild animals is typically a very private event. One reason for this, of course, is that during these moments of intimate bliss they are quite vulnerable to detection and capture by predators. It is one of the few occasions of outright distraction from their usual wariness. My naturalist's curiosity was piqued by this little sideshow of reproductive behavior and I quickly took my camera from my pack and photographed several stages of their mating activity.

The smaller male on top had his jaws clamped onto the females back-ward projecting horns. At the same time he was grappling and twisting the females' posterior upward, bringing their genitalia together for the insertion of the male's penis into the female's cloaca, her equivalent of the human vagina. I continued to observe and photograph the lizards for several minutes and then I left them alone to their love-making. My continued presence near the ferrug hawk nest was weighing heavily on my mind and I felt compelled to get out of their territory and end my disturbing intrusion.

At the time I wondered if the intimate mating behavior for this particular species, the desert horned lizard (*Phrynosoma platyrhinos*), had ever been observed or described before. Over the years since then, I have occasionally mentioned that observation to experienced herpetologists, biologists who study and know lizards and snakes, and asked them if they knew whether that particular facet of reproductive behavior is known for the species. Invariably, these scientist didn't know. Finally, while recently working on a short scientific note of a similar nature, I did a thorough search of the known information on this horned lizard and found no record of this aspect of behavior. Therefore, I made a small, natural addition to the paper that I was working on and included this old observation. With a couple of nicely done illustrations that my former student and good friend, Peter Gaede, produced from my old photographs, this little tidbit of missing lizard reproductive behavior has now been officially reported. It waited from 1972 until 2000, but this particular serendipitous lizard sideshow, "love in the sun" now rests in the herpetological literature.

Tarred and De-feathered

The La Brea Tar Pit is a prehistoric phenomenon well known to most of us today. A trip to the nearby Los Angeles County Museum can't help but impress one with the magnitude of entrapment and mortality that befell a vast array of resident fauna at that tar pit over the centuries. Certainly, the La Brea Tar Pit was about the farthest thing from my mind on the mid-March day that Rich Howard and I pulled into the little gravel-pit at the extreme south end of Black Pine Valley. What had caught our attention however, was a clump of feathers fluttering in the afternoon breeze at the edge of the pit. At a distance it looked like a dead hawk. Parking and walking over to the site we found a large patch of excess tar that the highway department had dumped over the edge on one side of the pit. The resultant flow streamed over the ground for nearly fifty yards and in some places was over ten feet wide. Viewing it close-up, we could see the remains of several bird carcasses embedded in the black sludge. One of the fresher, more recent, and more visible carcasses was obviously a ferruginous hawk. We counted fifteen other birds, with larger ones easily recognized as a northern harrier and several ravens. Smaller, sparrow-size birds appeared to be more completely immersed in the tar, making their identification nearly impossible. This was certainly one of the most unusual sources of mortality that we had discovered for ferrugs. In essence, we had found a miniature, modern-day La Brea Tar Pit. Like its larger, prehistoric name-sake, this little tar pit was taking a toll on wildlife, even if it was on a much smaller scale. Rich and I picked away at the encrusted tar around the ferrug carcass to see if the bird had a band on its leg. We found none. The tar was soft enough that we left our boot prints in its surface as we walked across it but at the time it wasn't sticky. Yet this was in March; still early spring. During the hot temperatures of summer, we could easily visualize the increased hazard posed by the melted tar.

We tried to reconstruct the deadly scenario that was probably at work here. After all, what bird in its "right mind" would be enticed to frolic around in oozing, black tar? As we walked about inspecting the tar flow, one possible reason for the wildlife's attraction to this spot became evident. From certain angles, the tar's surface gave off a water-like reflection. Ah ha, now we were getting somewhere! Bypassing critters could easily mistake this stream-like flow for water—a potentially deadly deception and enticement, especially to desert wildlife. That might explain their initial attraction to the tar flow, but it didn't seem to completely answer the question, why would these birds enter the tar, once they were up close? Closer inspection of portions of the tar flow provided us with some probable answers to that question too.

Scattered throughout the tar were embedded insects, of various sizes and shapes. Now, a plausible scenario for this whole death trap took shape. During the warmer months of the year when hot temperatures rendered this tar thinner and stickier, flying insects that were enticed to touch down on the water-like surface could easily get stuck. Once some of these decoyed flying insects became trapped, their helpless and conspicuous fluttering would most certainly attract small birds that normally prey on them. These small birds may or may not have been initially attracted to the water-like surface of the tar, and even if not prone to enter the tar, they'd likely fall victim while trying to recover the insects. The desperate fluttering movements of the entrapped small birds would provide even more conspicuous enticement to larger predators, especially aerial forms such as hawks and ravens who could spot these victims at greater distances.

Scavengers would also be drawn to the exposed dead carcasses, which might partly explain the presence of the several ravens in the tar. Like a black, sticky magnet the tar flow compressed the area food chain into its deadly mass.

This scenario of a modern, man-made tar pit and its entrapment and mortality to wildlife has been well documented numerous times in other areas and times. After Rich and I discovered the tar flow in our study area, I found references in the scientific literature documenting similar instances that dated back to the 1930s and 1940s. Apparently, once our society began paving our highways with tar-like petroleum-based asphalt, dumpsites for excess material have created these deadly traps, small as they are.

As I recall, Rich and I registered our complaints with the local highway authorities but I don't really know how much good it did. My last visit to the tar flow was four years later and although I don't think it had been added to, neither had it been covered with dirt or disposed of in any way. Birds were still being "tarred and de-feathered" at that site.

Water Tanks, Gang Planks, and Death by Drowning

It became increasingly apparent to me as I continued my study of hawks, just how many ways we humans can kill wildlife—even unintentionally, without any mal-intent. True, I did examine an occasional hawk that had been shot, quite intentionally. But I suspect that there was a far greater number of raptors that died as innocent victims of man-made contrivances or human activity. I found some smashed on the roads, after being struck down by the zooming four-wheeled "predator" against which their genes offered little protection. I also found evidence of some raptors mortally entangled in barbed wire fences. Good fences may make good neighbors but they can also make deadly obstacles for low-flying birds. Many of the chemicals that poison the food or thin the egg shells of raptors aren't directed to the hawks and owls themselves; the birds are simply innocent, "non-target" victims. Certainly, the tar flow episode was not an intentional trap laid out for any of the creatures that perished therein. But they perished, none-the-less. I guess our human proclivity is simply that of ignorance and an even greater lack of concern for the broader ramifications or consequences of our actions, especially as they might pertain to wildlife. During the third summer of my study, Tim and I stumbled onto yet another example of wildlife death by human negligence. Our discovery served ominous notice of a widespread and very insidious danger to smaller wildlife. What was that threat?

One day in early July we were making the rounds of several of the ferrug nests, banding as many of the nestlings as we could get our hands on. In between hawk nests, we happened to stop briefly at a livestock watering tank. This watering tank was one of many standard, fairly common tanks that were scattered throughout this desert countryside to provide spring-produced water to the livestock that grazed the open range. Water courses of any kind were few and far between out in this arid landscape, so these man-made tanks and troughs were often the only source of water for cattle, horses, or sheep. Most were circular, roughly sixteen feet in diameter, and less than two feet deep. Though the tank we inspected on that particular day was empty, we were surprised to find the partially decomposed remains of several birds laying in its bottom. Curious naturalists that we were, we crawled inside the tank and examined them more closely for identification. We easily recognized seven American kestrels, plus two other sparrow-size birds that were too badly decomposed to recognize. We were a bit shocked to find so many of these colorful little falcons dead in the tank. It immediately raised the question: how many more small birds might there be floating in the water or encrusted in the dried bottoms of the myriad of other stock tanks scattered about the countryside?

Before we left the study area that summer we were only able to check two other watering tanks but found remains of not only birds, but small mammals in them as well.

We found some other interesting evidence that suggested raptor activity around those two watering tanks. Portions of jackrabbits found in both tanks looked like they had been picked clean by raptors, suggesting that hawks or eagles used the tanks as feeding perches on which to sit while eating. The presence of burrowing owl castings or regurgitated pellets at two of the tanks indicated that they also sometimes used the tanks for perches. A raptor biologist from Colorado later told us that he knew of an adult female prairie falcon that had drowned in a watering tank. So, obviously, even though our sample size was small, there was no question that livestock watering tanks were posing a little known hazard to some small mammals and a variety of small to medium sized birds. But how could this happen? Although we were particularly curious about the raptor mortality that was occurring in these tanks, the loss of other animals bothered us too.

Disturbed by this potential wildlife death trap that we'd uncovered, Tim and I now wanted to figure out why and how these animals fell victim to their drowning, so that we might contemplate some means of preventing it. Interestingly, this man-made mode of inadvertently killing wildlife had some similarities to the tar flow incident that Rich and I had found two years earlier. Tim and I reasoned out the scenario of death at our watering tanks in similar fashion.

Raptors might enter these stock tanks for one of several reasons. The presence of castings and prey remains certainly indicated that some birds of prey use the tanks as feeding perches. That being the case, it is very possible that some raptors might be enticed to enter the water to retrieve dropped prey items and then be unable to extricate themselves. With water levels usually well below the top of the tank, the dunked birds with their water logged feathers would likely be doomed. For many of the desert animals, the water itself may be an alluring attraction to these stock tanks. Small rodents such as the deer mice (*Peromyscus maniculatus*) that we found in the tanks likely fell in by accident, trying to get to the water. They and the insects that also drown in the tanks could entice smaller birds, including some of the raptors such as the seven American kestrels that we found in one tank. And like the tar flow, the mechanics of the food chain probably operates to decoy larger raptor species in pursuit of floundering mice, smaller birds, etc. Thrashing movements of the drowning victims would trigger intense investigative and hunting behavior by raptors as well as other predators. Young raptors newly fledged from nearby nests would be very hungry and most vulnerable. It is even possible that many of the drowning victims are removed and eaten elsewhere by larger mammalian predators or scavengers such as foxes, coyotes, and bobcats, leaving no trace of the drowning victims—somewhat veiling the severity of this death trap.

Tim and I had no intention of running about the countryside screaming that the sky was falling, or crying wolf. But this accidental killing of wildlife had a potential of enormous magnitude! Imagine, if you will, the number of these watering tanks that are traditionally scattered across the entire arid and semi-arid West. Even if only half of them are drowning wildlife, it doesn't take a rocket scientist to arrive at the staggering numbers of dead critters. All Tim and I hoped to do was to create an awareness of the problem and encourage these stock tank users to implement some simple precautions that might alleviate the carnage. Most of these watering tanks resided on public grazing lands that were administered by the Bureau of Land Management (BLM) a Federal agency with responsibility for a certain degree of wildlife management. Certainly, we wanted to make that agency aware of the problem.

Not surprisingly, ranchers were already aware of the wildlife drownings in their watering tanks. We spoke with one rancher who stated that he drained his water tanks when they were not in use to prevent hawks from drowning in them, an occurrence he had seen several times. To their credit, I found the great majority of ranchers and farmers that I contacted were very observant, well meaning, hard working, friendly, and cooperative folks. Thus, I was not surprised at their awareness of the problem. But despite their lack of incentive to do so, I was still a little disappointed with their general disinterest in trying to remedy the problem—it wouldn't have taken much.

So what is the remedy to the watering tank death trap? When Tim and I later published a note on this problem in the ornithological journal *Condor* (Vol. 78, 1976), we suggested the most simple solution, that of floating a small plank in the tank, thus facilitating escape from the water for trapped victims. We hoped that such a remedy might stop these drownings, yet impose the least effort and expenditure for ranchers. Obviously, an even better solution would be to construct a small escape ramp of some sort. We didn't even propose that method, presuming that it entailed way too much work and expense to ever be popular among the livestock people. Surprisingly, in recent years I have noticed a widespread change in design of some water troughs that include a built-in ramp at one end to allow escape for trapped victims. What has surprised me even more, is that I still find drowned birds and other small animals in those "ramped" tanks—but that's another story for another book. To this day, Tim and I still occasionally ponder and discuss possible new solutions to water tanks, gang planks, and death by drowning.

Wild Dogs

Given the bad blood that I'd witnessed between ferruginous hawks and coyotes, I was intrigued by the unusual presence of "coyote cousins" at one of my hawk nests. This particular nest site was the same place where the great horned owl killed and ate the short-eared owl one night during my moonlight vigil. The hawks had labored long and hard that spring constructing a nest in a row of trees that divided two alfalfa fields. Because it was one of the few ferrug nests that I knew of that resided on cultivated farmland, I kept it under close observation that spring and summer. I was curious to find out just how resilient this shy hawk species is to the fairly high level of human activity that typically occurs on farmland—such as the irrigators on motor bikes, tractors, hay trucks, and pickup trucks that worked around this nest.

It was mid-April, when the resident hawks were about ready to lay their eggs and begin incubation, that I first noticed unexpected visitors from a nearby farmhouse. I was watching the hawks from the attic of a rickety old abandoned barn nearly 200 yards from the row of trees that contained the hawk nest. Around ten-thirty in the morning a pair of farm dogs wandered into view. Through my spotting scope I could tell that one, of black Labrador descent, was a lactating bitch. Traveling with her was a black and white spotted male Australian Shepherd. The dogs disappeared somewhere behind the barn and I lost sight of them and thought little more about them. At first I thought they might move out into the hayfield closer to the hawk nest, in which case, I would be curious to see the hawks reaction to their presence. But the dogs never reappeared that day.

Because these hawks were at the incubation stage of their nesting cycle and thus activity was at a real slowdown, I made no more observations at that nest site for nearly a month. When I finally returned in mid-May and spent most of a morning recording activity at this farmland nest, the two dogs again appeared. As before, the black Lab bitch and her Australian Shepherd companion traveled together. This time they passed on beyond the barn in which I was hiding, and they continued out into the field toward the nest. A short distance from the barn they stopped and sniffed the air, and I wondered if perhaps they had caught my scent. Since I first saw these dogs, nearly a month ago, I had discovered where they lived. Several times during the past month while driving by this farmstead I noticed these two dogs hanging around the base of an old abandoned farmhouse a quarter mile up the road from this hawk nest. Apparently, they were rag-tag dogs, abandoned and living on their own. I couldn't help but feel sorry for them and thought that surely the neighboring farmers must have known about them.

This morning the dogs continued further out into the field and appeared to be hunting, occasionally darting about, sniffing the ground, and sometimes digging briefly. Though it was still early in the nesting season, I knew there were either eggs or young to protect in the hawk nest, and I grew immediately interested in how the ferrugs might respond to these canine intruders—especially knowing their hostility toward coyotes.

Nearly two hours earlier the male hawk had brought a small rodent to the female at the nest and she had taken the food, flown out and landed in the field, and began eating. After his mate's departure the male stepped down into the nest and settled low. It appeared that these birds were still incubating, as the male was sitting low in the nest. Usually, the attending adults sat higher in the nest once they were brooding or covering chicks instead of eggs. This "changing of the guard" was common after a food delivery by the male, and offered the female hawk some time away from the nest to stretch, defecate, feed, and preen. From all of my observations, the male ferrug incubated about thirty percent of the time, usually following food exchanges like this. Thus, the female ferrugs did most of the incubation and virtually all of the brooding of young chicks. In this instance, perhaps the male's incubation duties diverted him from responding defensively, but neither hawk seemed to pay much attention to the hunting dogs in their territory.

As I watched the dogs through the spotting scope, I was amazed to see the black bitch suddenly snap her head up with a pocket gopher in her jaws. She immediately laid down and ate the rodent. Her Aussie mate was nearby engrossed in similar hunting activity although I never saw him capture or eat anything. Less than five minutes later I again watched the black dog catch and eat what appeared to be another gopher. By this time the spotted male had worked his way nearly fifty yards to the west to an old carcass of a dead cow. He now appeared to be tugging and eating at the carcass. Obviously these dogs were hungry and fending for themselves!

Both hawks were sitting tight—the male on the nest, the female on her break, perched on the ground some 200 yards from the foraging dogs. I contented myself with watching the hunting exhibition being masterfully demonstrated by the black bitch. Soon, I witnessed her third gopher catch. In the space of barely twenty minutes she had successfully captured and eaten three gophers! With my attention somewhat divided between watching the hawks and the dogs, I could easily have missed other successful captures by the bitch. I couldn't help but wonder if the two resident ferruginous hawks might benefit by observing and taking lessons from this dog! Though I had watched these hawks hunt these same fields for many days, I couldn't remember ever seeing the hawks capture gophers with such regularity and in such rapid succession. Of course, the hawks were considerably smaller and hardly had the appetite of a black Lab. But it was a good reminder to me that our domesticated canine friends are not all that far removed from their *Canis* wolf-like forebearers. They still had the keen edge of hunting instincts and survival when forced to rely upon them.

That day the two dogs continued on across the field and eventually disappeared near the road that bordered the field to the west. I suspected that they eventually returned to their home at the old abandoned farmhouse where the female could tend to her pups.

Four days later on my return to that hawk nest, the black female spent part of the evening hunting the field between me and the hawk nest in much the same manner as she had done before. I was so engrossed in the heightened hawk activity now that they were feeding young, I couldn't track her hunting success as I had done previously but I had no doubt that she knew what she was doing and was probably faring well on gophers, as were her pups. I never saw her spotted mate that evening.

Based upon the number of times that I saw these dogs hunting within the hawk's territory, on my infrequent observation visits, they must have made regular hunting forays through the area. I think that was borne out by the facility with which the black bitch caught gophers which, due to their highly subterranean existence, are not easy prey to capture. The presence of the old cow carcass apparently provided occasional meals, especially to the Australian Shepherd, and likely held some attraction to the dogs for repeated visits. If so, perhaps it was this somewhat regular presence of dogs in the territory that fostered the lack of defense against them by the hawks. Also, maybe the dogs' appearance—color and demeanor—was far enough removed from that coyote image that they simply didn't trigger the hawks' instinctive response. In any case, this little vignette by the two cast-away farm dogs was not only instructional to me as a naturalist but equally entertaining as an observer. I also suspect that in Curlew Valley gopher-dom some subterranean burrows still occasionally reverberate with rodent horror stories of the "Black Bitch and her Aussie Mate"!

17

The Hawk, the Swoop, and the Hare are One

Patiently watching hawk activity at different nests day after day taught me a lot about ferrug family life but my ringside seat at the nest offered little opportunity to see much of their hunting. My peeping-tom study approach simply kept me too close to their home. Throughout much of the nesting season, capturing food was the province of the male hawk and often took him considerable distance away from the nest, well out of view from my blinds. I had a pretty good idea of *what* the hawks were hunting, for I watched quite a number of prey deliveries at several nests and found plenty of food remains at others. It was simply that too little of that hunting occurred close enough at hand for me to observe *where* or *how* they actually obtained their food.

Swooping onto the nest edge with food in his talons, the male hawk usually paused only momentarily before departing. Sometimes he'd glide softly off to a nearby favorite perch and sit briefly, glancing around before taking leave of the area. Territorial duty seemed to call strongly and soon he'd wing his way low over the sage then begin ringing slowly upward, lofted by unseen updrafts that he knew so well but I could only imagine. All too soon his ethereal soar would dissolve into the oblivion of fluffy clouds and sunlit sky. So many times my spirit wanted to join him and soar into his secret world of stealth, surveillance, and capturing of prey. But alas, I remained pinned to the earth, contenting myself with spying into the private home life of his mate and offspring. Nest life was my priority of study. None-the-less, though well out of sight, the distant male often revisited my thoughts as I peered from the portals of my blind and frequently pondered his whereabouts and activity. Though ferrug food habits were not the focus of my research, and nesting behavior was, yet, to successfully nest, these hawks needed ample nutrition. So, I still hoped to learn something about the role of the adults in acquiring their food. Successful hunting seemed closely linked to successful nesting.

One exception to this absentee hunter dilemma was just north of Snowville at the Old Barn Nest situated in a windrow between alfalfa fields. There, the abundance of pocket gophers, a common scourge in agricultural fields, so encircled the nest site that the ferrugs practically hunted from their doorstep. I'm sure it was also this human-induced bounty of farmland rodents that shrank the entire scope of the male hawk's activity into its smallish oval territory, barely covering the 160 acres of alfalfa. Open fields inhabited by gophers galore at this nest gave me close and easy viewing of lots of hunting action. Day after day I watched the male hawk regularly pluck pocket gophers and voles from the hayfields. However, in the end I had to rely on the accounts of other observers to learn how the hawks hunted their primary prey, jackrabbits. And even those eye-witness accounts were practically non-existent.

It was also at the Old Barn ferrug territory that it became increasingly clear to me that even if the female hawk had ample opportunity to hunt close to the nest, as was the case there, she rarely did. Instead, she maintained her nest-side vigil of her eggs or young, leaving it to her mate to provide food. Apparently, the ancient patterns of parental protection were stamped so deeply into the female's behavioral fabric that even a cornucopia of gophers could not entice her from that ingrained rhythm of behavior. At other times of the year, elemental hunger would propel her readily skyward in search of food. But now that magical mix of day length, genes, and hormones bound her to the greater and unremitting magnetism of her nest and its contents. Only later, after young hawks were out of the nest did the female resume hunting.

So what is the main fare in the diet of ferruginous hawks? How versatile are they in subsisting on the available food in their remote landscapes? Given the widespread and long-standing public perception of hawks as predatory vermin, especially within agricultural circles, I was somewhat surprised to find ferrugs free of any reputed villainy as "chicken hawks". More surprisingly, this vindication from poultry skulduggery dates back a very long time. As early as 1900, in the Big Sky country of Montana, E.S. Cameron maintained this hawk's innocence and even offered proof from a neighboring rancher who for sixteen years protected several nesting pairs of ferrugs on his ranch. Despite their frequent flights over the buildings, throughout all those years the hawks never molested the rancher's chickens.

Ferrugs do eat birds; why not chickens? I'm tempted to think that the remote localities of most ferrug nests have probably isolated them from run-ins with chicken farmers. In those out-of-the-way places, hawks likely encounter few enticements for perfidy with domestic fowl. Yet, even some of those remote localities sported prairie-chicken cousins, the sharp-tailed grouse (*Tympanuchus phasianellus*) and greater sage grouse (*Centrocercus urophasianus*) that ferrugs are known to have occasionally dined on. None-the-less, despite their natural, occasional taste for these chickens of the prairie, ferrugs seem to have kept their beaks clean around the barnyard fowl and enjoy a remarkably unblemished reputation with farmers and ranchers.

Bird hunting is always a challenge, to which some hunter-type readers can readily attest. Even among raptors it is left to a select few. Among the hawks, bird hunting usually falls to the agile and highly maneuverable *Accipiters*, like the northern goshawk (*Accipiter gentilis*), Cooper's hawk (*A. cooperii*) and sharp-shinned hawk (*A. striatus*), all residents of wooded terrain where they hunt from cover by stealth and bursts of speed in ambush of unsuspecting prey. Most speedy falcons can also do a number on birds, as the old moniker "duck hawk" for the peregrine falcon (*Falco perigrinus*) readily at-tests. Of course, the sleek and more fleet falcons pre-fer the open country and needn't bother so much with stealth nor be much concerned about unsus-pecting prey; they simply out-fly the avian victims and strike them to the ground. The slower, broad-winged *Buteos*, however, are not so well equipped for catching birds, especially on the wing. Most of their successful attacks are on unsuspecting stationary targets. So, it comes as no big surprise that in the overall picture of ferrug food habits, birds simply have never been a big item in the hawk's diet. The western meadowlark *(Sternella neglecta)*, sharp-tailed grouse, horned lark *(Eremophila alpestris)*, black-billed magpie *(Pica pica)*, long-billed curlew *(Numenius americanus)*, and, in recent years, ring-necked pheasants *(Phasianus colchicus)* are among the common bird neighbors occasionally falling prey to this hawk. And even the majority of these avian prey are more likely to be immature individuals, probably less wary and more stationary as targets—in other words, easy pickin's. Tim Craig and I on separate occasions watched flying ferrugs dipping and kiting shallowly over adult long-billed curlews on the ground below, as if testing them as potential prey; perhaps also checking for scrambling young birds that would be easier targets.

Interestingly, it was on that same Montana ranch mentioned above, that Cameron also describes one of the few known ferrug attacks on a domestic animal. Scattered piles of lumber that occupied a small sector of the ranch harbored quite a number of cottontail rabbits, which the resident ferrugs occasionally hunted, as did, also, one of the ranch housecats. Pondering that situation for just a moment, can you begin to see the potential for a "cat—astrophe" occurring there?

One day while the ranch owner and his foreman stood in conversation near a pile of posts on which the housecat lay basking in the sun, a ferrug that was hunting over the area suddenly dove and picked up the cat, lofting it twenty-five feet into the air before the tabby was able to twist about, clawing, spitting, and screaming with enough resistance that the hawk dropped it. The cat landed safely, and ducked under cover of the nearest woodpile. Most likely in this case the cat was mistaken for a cottontail but wielded a bit more startling, predatory weaponry against the hawk than expected from a rabbit—and thus it escaped.

Its impossible to know if this "cat—astrophe" experience caused the hawk any future suspicion of rabbits, but humorously, thereafter, all the rancher had to do was throw his hat into the air and the skittish kitty would immediately panic and dash for cover. It had become quite leery of largish flying objects!

The occasional avian appetizer aside, it is their main fare of rodents and rabbits that sustains ferrug populations throughout their range. In exactly which order of abundance, rodents or rabbits, depends somewhat on the neighborhood population cycles of each, as well as on the particular portion of the ferrug's range. Major food items may vary from prairie dogs that still occur on the eastern side of the hawk's range, to ground squirrels, jackrabbits, and cottontails that prevail more to the west. Population highs and lows fluctuate along three to four year cycles for common vole or field mouse species, but jackrabbits show longer, eight to ten year intervals between peaks. Ground squirrels and pocket gophers seem less bound to population cycles, remaining more universally present.

The former name of "Squirrel Hawk" in parts of its range attests to the ferrug's liking for ground squirrels and prairie dogs. In 1914

Cameron described how these hawks liked to perch on the ground amid prairie dog towns in a patient wait-and-take strategy. Inevitably one of the large rodents would venture too far out from its burrow, and the ferrug would wing quickly after it, sometimes succeeding in intercepting it before it could reach the safety of home. At the Old Barn territory, the male hawk sometimes hunted pocket gophers from the ground. Unlike ground squirrels or prairie dogs, gophers are far less active above ground and therefore considerably less visible. The hawks' strategy was to perch on the ground next to a burrow entrance or on top of fresh mounds. There they'd sit intently watching the dirt piles in front of them, perhaps listening as well. Those vigils at the mounds occasionally culminated in a sudden pounce and snag of a gopher by the hawk. Though highly subterranean, seldom appearing completely on the surface, this Idaho gopher species, valley pocket gopher, (*Thomomys townsendii*) does frequently push excavated dirt out of the open burrow's entrance, at that time partially exposing itself to the outside world, and predators. The generally high frequency of pocket gophers in ferrug food habit studies bears testimony to both, busy pocket gophers and the hawks' hunting success.

The real heavyweight in the ferrugs' diet is literally the jackrabbit, more commonly the black-tailed species (*Lepus californicus*) but in some areas also the larger white-tailed jackrabbit (*Lepus townsendii*). Even though the ferrug is North America's largest hawk, taking these fast food heavyweights is a truly remarkable feat.

To better understand what I mean, let me offer several reminders about predators. First, recognize that the life of a predator daily oscillates somewhere between feast and famine. Their lifestyle is precarious and regularly requires the pursuit, attack, and overpowering of an unwilling victim, sometimes larger than they. And don't forget, the prey, or intended victim is not normally inclined toward complacency about the predator's threat on its life. It isn't inclined to "roll-over and play dead". Typically, a predator grapples with a victim that is fighting for its life, biting, kicking, clawing, scratching for survival—often screaming in terror and agony as well. In short, predation is a feat of arms for most vertebrate predators. Arguably, such is the case for the ferruginous hawk that successfully preys on jackrabbits. Because these large hares outweigh most hawks, and are fairly renowned kick-boxing specialists, their avian predators are primarily the larger ferrug and eagles. Of course, night-wandering hares —desert jackrabbits or forest-dwelling snowshoe hares—had better also be on the lookout for that night-stalker, the great horned owl.

Despite the fact that jackrabbits may weigh between four and eight pounds, the three to four pound ferrug has long experienced the best of livelihoods by skillfully taking these hefty hares as prey. Ferrug food habit records and their periodic population peaks throughout the West bear testimony to this. The common scene of numerous rabbit remains, including the occasional occurrence of entire adult jackrabbit carcasses at ferrug nests attest to the strength and hunting prowess of this hawk. However, for the myriad of dead jackrabbits that have littered ferrug nests since time immemorial, eyewitness accounts of this hawk's capturing a rabbit are pitifully few. But then, when was the last time you saw *any* act of predation?

Throughout the cycle of the seasons, for all the countless acts of predation which naturally and necessarily occur hourly, daily, across our wilder landscapes, it remarkably eludes human attention. This is partially due to our current human predicament in which we are sufficiently disconnected from nature. Typically, our urban or suburban mindsets insulate us from the notion of predation, while our neatly manicured settings further isolate us from its reality. If you're observant, perhaps you've occasionally noticed the backyard robin extracting and tenderizing an earthworm from your lawn. Particularly keen observers may even rarely witness the hovering roadside kestrel suddenly plummet to the freeway median and lift off with a grasshopper or mouse clutched in its feet. These suburban-rural snippets of full-daylight predation, or something similar, is probably the extent of most human experiences in witnessing wild food chains in action.

But our culturally induced imperceptivity of nature is not entirely to blame for this commonplace ignorance of predatory acts. We mustn't forget that the predator is a hunter. The prerequisite stealth and swiftness so often accompanying acts of predation also make it difficult to witness. This is especially true of airborne predators where speed and angle of attack, by intent, is an elusive hunting strategy, and barely perceptible. That is why the prey may be taken by surprise: the oncoming attack eludes their attention too; at least until it is probably too late. Accordingly, there are few eyewitness accounts of ferrugs killing jackrabbits.

Occasional observers have suggested that these hawks hunt in pairs, perhaps cooperatively, with one hawk working low over the sagebrush while its mate circles high overhead. Anything flushed by the lower bird may then be ambushed from above. Recalling my opening account of the cooperative attack on a coyote by the adult pair of hawks in defense of their nestlings, teaming-up on prey certainly seems plausible.

One researcher described watching a ferrug chase a jackrabbit that escaped into a dense clump of sagebrush. Landing, the hawk followed into the brush on foot, flushed the rabbit back out into the open, took wing and quickly captured it. That kind of ground pursuit really shouldn't surprise anyone. Perhaps with exception of its open tundra dwelling cousin of the far north, the rough-legged hawk, the ferrug is the ground dweller of the western *buteos*—perching, hunting, feeding, gathering nesting material, and sometimes even nesting on the ground. It is certainly no stranger to *terra firma*. They seem to occupy ground perches with the same proclivity as atop junipers or as regularly as they soar in the updrafts of desert thermals. They are often seen standing on open ground like stately white sentinels of their shrub-grass domain.

A quick kill is to the predator's advantage. The sooner the prey is immobilized or dispatched, the less chance it has to inflict any injury to the predator —this is especially true of larger prey. As a hawk strikes its prey, the force of the impact helps to drive the talons deeply into its victim, afflicting mortal damage, usually into vital areas. In most cases a prolonged grasp on the smaller prey is sufficient to kill them fairly quickly. When seizing larger quarry many raptors continue working their feet and deadly talons with a rapid series of alternating, impaling clutches, effectively perforating and hastening the demise of its victim. Even a rabbit usually succumbs to this predatory efficiency in short order.

It is not uncommon for a hawk to begin feeding almost immediately after its victim ceases to struggle, and shows the first signs of death. Mantling with wings half-spread over its prey, quick, tearing bites are interspersed with nervous, watchful glances around its surroundings. Though very intent on its prize, while perched on the ground with food the hawk seems to sense its extreme vulnerability to other predators, and the prospect of having its meal stolen, or being attacked themselves. For the ferrug, such neighborhood dangers might include other large raptors like the golden eagle, or hungry earth-bound predators like coyotes, foxes, bobcats, and badgers.

After some minutes of feeding and recouping its energy, the hawk usually turns its attention to transporting the quarry to its family waiting back at the nest. The male hawk and the jackrabbit have just fulfilled their age-old destinies, as expressed so succinctly yet eloquently in the words of some poet:

"The hawk,
the swoop,
and the hare are one."*

* Caldwell, William A. 1978. "Hawk and Hare are One". *Bird Watcher's Digest* 1(1):61-62.

Over the years, my experience with ferrugs has persuaded me that in their western range amid desert shrub-land, they dine at their best and live most securely on jackrabbits. My reasoning is based upon the observed relationship between high jackrabbit population levels and greater number of successful nesting pairs of ferrugs; as well as the higher number of young hawks produced in those nests. Adequate numbers of jackrabbits have shown me healthier ferrug nesting populations with larger clutches of young per nest. Low jackrabbit populations resulted in fewer pairs of ferrugs attempting to nest, and fewer young produced in those remaining successful nests. I saw evidence of that trend across the Little and Big Lost River Valleys to the north as well as down in the Curlew, Black Pine, and Raft River Valleys of my main study area. Early in my study, with rabbits aplenty, nearly 90 percent of 48 nesting pairs of ferrugs laid eggs. Four young birds per nest and even occasionally five were not uncommon that summer. By the next nesting season the jackrabbit population had crashed, resulting in very low numbers of rabbits. That kind of sudden population collapse is fairly typical of these lagomorphs. Even though Rich Howard and I had discovered a few additional nesting sites by the second year of our study, roughly half of 54 ferrug nesting pairs were incapable of producing eggs, and even those productive nests had fewer young, usually only two or three. Sure, ferrugs survive during those rabbit lows but in my opinion they live by the law of the minimum—a precarious existence, especially today, in the face of radical changes sweeping much of their habitat. Those changes I discuss in the

Epilogue, but my point here is that abundant jack-rabbits bode well for ferrugs.

Living with ferruginous hawks as I did during a jackrabbit population collapse, laid bare some of the subtleties of this hawk's hunting habits. For example, after the rabbits disappeared I saw a lot of small-sized, alternate quarry delivered to the nest, to be quickly gulped down whole by hungry nestlings. This consumption of small, alternate prey leaves no detectable remains for cataloging by food habits researchers. From my blinds, however, I was privy to those obscure daily occurrences and even recorded many on film. Lizards, such as the western whiptail (*Cnemodophorus tigris*), desert horned (*Phrynosoma platyrhinos*), and long-nosed leopard lizard (*Gambelia wislizenii*), were all delivered and quickly eaten during my watch at the nests. Other lizards native to the area were probably also taken—possibly in my absence. Outside my study area, I've also seen gopher snake (*Pituophis melanoleucus*) remains in nests. In the absence of rabbits, larger sized snakes certainly offer more food per catch than do the smaller, lizard reptiles.

Another smaller prey that I saw delivered to the nests on several occasions, often at mid-day, shed further light on the ferrug's hunting habits. Kangaroo rats (k-rats) (*Dipodomys ordii*), weighing barely more than a lizard, made more frequent appearances among captured prey than one would expect for a nocturnal rodent. Neither Rich nor I noticed them among prey remains in the hawk nests the first year of our study. It wasn't until the next summer, after the rabbit population crash, that we first noticed k-rats in some of the nests. For a little rodent that scampers around at night, the k-rats' appearance in the food habits of a daytime hawk was a bit puzzling and posed the obvious question: *when* did the ferrugs hunt them? Like a lot of nocturnal animals, k-rats will venture out a little early and begin their activity before dark—during the crepuscular or twilight time. That was most likely when a late-hunting ferrug had opportunity to snatch one. And ferrugs do remain active late into the evening.

Yet, k-rat prey still provoked the notion that just maybe, ferrugs hunted these ubiquitous desert rodents under the nighttime light of the full moon. That was the question that prompted my moonlight vigil I describe in Chapter 9 (Winged Marauders of the Night) at the Old Barn Nest—the only nest site at which I could regularly watch the hawks hunt. Though there were few k-rats there, I knew that pocket gophers remained active through the night and also might possibly entice moonlit night hunting—though I saw no evidence of it during my moonlight vigil.

Even more peculiar about these k-rat rations were the odd times of the day at which they were brought to the nests—in many cases mid-day or mid-afternoon. Certainly, the nocturnal k-rats were not being captured at those times. Instead, the hawks must have caught the rodents during the twilight of dusk or dawn and then stashed them until later, a practice known as food caching or hoarding behavior. Predators sometimes intensify their hunting of sporadically abundant prey during the peak activity periods, stashing surplus victims in a convenient hiding place, then retrieving them later when hunger or family food demands warrant it. This provides a more constant food supply even during later daily lulls of prey activity. Food caching is a fairly widespread practice among raptors. Probably other prey species were also cached between the times they were caught and brought to the nest—it was simply more noticeable with k-rats.

So, in the end those little kangaroo rats tipped me off to three of the ferrugs' hunting secrets. First, in the absence of larger bread and butter prey such as rabbits, k-rats suffice as an important backup "buffer species" to help them eke out at least a minimal nesting effort. Second, ferrugs must have hunted the twilight, crepuscular, hours in order to tap into this rodent's activity period. And lastly, the pre-darkness/predawn k-rat captures were often cached somewhere temporarily and delivered to the nest later in the day. All this was not a bad exposé for such a tiny rodent of the night.

Once I became aware of this caching behavior I wondered where the hawks stashed those excess prey items until they were needed. How far from the nest, and in what sort of a hiding place? Did they get around to retrieving all the stashed prey before the summer day's heat spurred decomposition to the point of spoilage? I personally never had the opportunity to explore or answer any of those questions but a few clues were offered by a couple of observations by Tony Angell in the sagebrush country of Washington State. While observing a nesting pair of ferrugs late one June he noticed the male hawk make a couple of flights from the same clump of sagebrush; the second, with part of a jackrabbit. Curious, Tony inspected the spot, which was about 350 yards from the nest. There he discovered what appeared to be a cache for prey. A short passage through the grass opened into a small sagebrush covert that contained lower portions of two jackrabbits, fresh enough to have been taken that morning. A check of the cache late the next afternoon found it empty. Regrettably, at that same time young ferrugs fledged from the nest and no further information was obtained concerning the cache site.

One last little oddity of ferrug hunting habits is probably such a rarity that it's hardly worth mentioning except that it illustrates so well the extreme hunting versatility of this large hawk. Though no expert at catching birds in flight, or hunting after dark, years ago ferrugs were one of several raptor species observed catching Brazilian free-tailed bats (*Tadarida braziliensis*) at Carlsbad Caverns National Park as the clouds of bats poured out of the cave just before dark. It certainly wasn't a common occurrence. To be exact, ferrugs were only seen hunting the bats on four out of 196 consecutive evening observations between May 1 and November 12, 1944. None-the-less, they did hunt bats and were successful. Not surprisingly, *Buteos* were only half as efficient as the bird specialist *Accipiters* in catching those bats, but even at that, the ferrug had a higher "batting average" or success rate than red-tails.

In a much varied yet repeating refrain, the hawk, the swoop, and the timeless ripple of energy spews from desert creatures into the lifeblood of the ferruginous hawk. It's a strange harmony but its cadence is eternal. Throughout this chapter I've intentionally refrained from rendering this hunting topic into a long, meticulous list of food items documented for this hawk. For surely that composite list is quite lengthy. Instead, I've tried to present an overview of some representative prey and hunting styles that ferrugs commandeer in their quiet quest for survival. It's also important to acknowledge that larger quarry constitute literally more "take-home-prey" and, like increased take-home-pay for you and me, it offers the ferruginous hawk better odds for success—as a family unit and as a species. Note that I use the word success, rather than survival. There is a difference. Survival on skimpy buffer species rations may assure that the *individual* lives another day, week or month but nesting and offspring are greatly in question. In contrast, rabbits or prairie dogs aplenty, bestows to the hawk another *generation* of numerous fledglings winging their way into the future population.

In a strange irony, this hawk that regularly duels with the sun, at the same time is fueled by the sun. An unseen solar-powered march of photosynthetic molecules, landscape-wide in magnitude, veritably flows from the soil upward through the roots and stalks of desert plants, exuding energy and life into the rabbit; pooled there for the taking by the hawk. The molecular odyssey continues as it infuses life into the blood and body of baby ferrugs. They grow hale and hearty—robust in stature as well as population number. This molecular tide measures out the hawks' energy and in due course, its future. In reality—

> the hawk,
> **the sun,**
> the swoop,
> and the hare are one.

EPILOGUE

This book about the ferruginous hawk is timely, even though I decided to write it long after my three-year sojourn with the birds. Without doubt, during the next decade or two of this new millennium, the general public will suddenly become aware of this heretofore obscure hawk. I fully expect that for the first time ever, its name is going to be bantered about the household news along with those of the Canada lynx, grizzly bear, and sage grouse. And like these other denizens of wild country, the ferruginous hawk is going to be a topic of concern for survival. In short, I think it is destined to be listed as a threatened species.

Throughout this book I have shared numerous examples of this species' struggle for survival against formidable natural odds. And I have been pleased to report that despite its running battles with coyotes, golden eagles, great horned owls, and the searing desert sun, the ferruginous hawk prevails more often than it fails. It is amazingly versatile in its feeding and nesting habits. It is one of the more prolific of the large hawks in its potential for producing large numbers of young. So, what could possibly be lurking on the horizon that might threaten its survival?

Actually, the hawk's status throughout its range has been debated for several decades. As I began my studies, the U.S. Fish and Wildlife Service was placing the ferruginous hawk in the "status undetermined" category because of its general anonymity. At that time, no one had a clue about its numbers and population status. Later, during the 1980s, the species was listed as a "species of special concern" in some parts of its range. Then, as recently as 1990, the species was listed as "threatened" by Canada. It had already been under consideration for similar listing in the United States. It has recently been listed as "threatened" in the State of Washington.

Although many different populations of ferruginous hawks have been studied over the past twenty-five years, only a very small portion (roughly one to two percent) of the naturally occurring populations have been monitored very consistently. Consequently, some areas report drastic declines in ferruginous hawk numbers while others show increases. However, throughout its entire range, there is so little consistent monitoring that it is impossible to know the species' over-all population status. Some biologists suspect that the population is still in decline.

The problem of estimating overall population levels is exacerbated by some evidence that ferruginous hawks may be somewhat nomadic, meaning that when prey levels become low in traditional nesting territories, the resident hawks move elsewhere to more favorable nesting areas. That may result in misleading "increases" in population levels in some areas, which in truth could simply be a reflection or measure of "losses" or vacant territories elsewhere. The question remains: Is a bubble in the population level merely a result of hawks being squeezed around from one place to another? Until more widespread and consistent monitoring of ferruginous hawk populations throughout the species' range is conducted for long periods, its true status will likely never be clearly known.

So why do I think the public is going to hear about concerns for this hawk's survival in the next couple of decades? Especially since we apparently don't really know whether this hawk is in trouble or not? It isn't because particular predators might eat ferruginous hawk eggs or young, or kill the adults themselves. Nor is it the absence of suitable nesting structures that worries me. In fact, because this hawk can subsist on such a variety of prey, I really don't expect the species to completely disappear from its range.

The issue is habitat. The ferruginous hawk, as a species, is tied to the sagebrush-perenial grass ecosystem, and that is in peril of being reduced drastically or even completely destroyed. That fact is at the very heart of the problem facing this hawk. Virtually all of its primary prey species reside in that ecosystem. Perhaps most importantly, healthy expanses of sagebrush shelter and produce healthy populations of black-tailed jackrabbits, which in turn support large and healthy populations of large raptors like ferruginous hawks and golden eagles. In short, I believe that ferruginous hawks fare better where substantial jackrabbit populations exist than where the birds must subsist on non-rabbit prey.

It's simply a matter of conserving energy. A foraging hawk's "take-home prey" is heftier per expenditure of time and energy when it is a jackrabbit instead of a lizard. Snagging and bringing home most of a jackrabbit carcass promises far greater nutritional value than does a lizard, kangaroo rat, or even a ground squirrel.

Not only is this economics of food and energy beneficial to the whole family, but it likely diminishes the "absentee male" syndrome: the amount of time males are forced to hunt farther away from the nest and for longer periods of time. This may be as important as food value, because in the perilous world of the ferruginous hawk, an absentee parent is as undesirable as are "dead-beat dads" in our society. The more available the male is to defend his territory, mate, nest, and young, the better are the family's odds of survival.

Ultimately the more families of ferruginous hawks that survive, the greater the overall population numbers will be. I believe that ferruginous hawks survive better in healthy, jackrabbit-infested sagebrush-perennial grass ecosystems than outside of them. Although some ferruginous populations exist on the Great Plains at the eastern edge of ferrug range and do not occupy typical shrub-steppe (sagebrush) habitat, the heart of this species' range is shrub-steppe.

We know that the sagebrush ecosystem is vanishing at the rate of hundreds of thousands of acres per year. This does not bode well for a number of wildlife species. Not only are ferruginous hawk numbers likely to decline, but any other species closely tied to sagebrush is destined for an even more precarious existence. It is no accident that the names of several of the most obvious candidates for "threatened" classification hint of sagebrush: sage grouse, sage thrashers, sage sparrows, sagebrush lizard, and so on.

Undoubtedly, there will be less public outcry over the demise of the song birds and the lizard, but perhaps we can depend on the gunners of upland game birds to muster enough political clout to protect habitat for the large, beautiful sage grouse. That is one of the ironies of wildlife politics—we'll make an effort to conserve "game animals" so our children can continue to kill them! Therefore, you will probably hear more concern expressed for sage grouse populations than you will for sage thrashers, pygmy rabbits, or ferruginous hawks. But the fate of these sagebrush species will ride the destiny coattails of the game species—either to recovery or to dim memories of the glory days of the past.

How is it possible that something as dominating and widespread as sagebrush in western North America could be threatened? After all, even in our lifetime, we Westerners have all driven through seemingly unending, monotonous stretches of sagebrush. How could all that grey-green vegetation possibly disappear? Well, it's literally going up in smoke. In the Great Basin alone, it is reported that range fires consumed two million acres of this habitat in 1999. In Idaho, up to seventy percent of the shrub-steppe community has been lost in recent years. Extend that potential to other parts of the West and extrapolate back a decade or two and you begin to get a feel for the magnitude of the problem.

But, you ask, won't it grow back after the fire? Unfortunately, a complicating factor continues to exacerbate rangefire peril. Fire alone is not the real nemesis of sagebrush communities. Fire has been around from the first thunderstorm. Fire is a natural part of the environment and historically played an important part in the dynamics of maintaining a natural mixture of sagebrush, shrubs and perennial bunchgrass in the ecosystem. The frequent fires touched off by lightning from summer thunderstorms were typically small, opening up patches of shrub habitat to the establishment of native perennial bunch grasses on a small scale, creating a mosaic or patchwork of shrub and grass communities. Recurring fires on these grassy patches burned slowly and were cool because of the wide spacing of the bunchgrass—a minor fire retardant and built-in safeguard against big, hot fires. Consequently, large catastrophic fires, although present, were apparently rare, which preserved vast stretches of sagebrush ecosystem. One has only to read the accounts of early travelers to capture an image of the overwhelming vastness of the sagebrush or "wormwood" habitat they saw as they crossed the West.

In our current crisis, an invading accomplice perverts and elevates the natural fire cycle into a catastrophic demon. The culprit is an introduced species known as cheatgrass (*Bromus tectorum*). Accidentally carried into our country more than a century ago as a contaminant in grain shipments, this grass rapidly spread across the West, encouraged by overgrazing, drought, agricultural practices, and natural and human-caused fires. Quickly, the vast expanses of sagebrush became fragmented by fires and subsequent infestations of cheatgrass, which was able to steal moisture from and out-compete the perennial grass and sagebrush seedlings.

Cheatgrass is an annual plant that forms a dense carpet of fine grass in spring. It soon dries and becomes highly flammable early in the summer. Ignited by lightning from thunderstorms, an area infested with cheatgrass burns and re-burns. Fire spreads to adjacent shrubs, opening more and more of the landscape to the quickly recovering cheatgrass. Soon, shrub patches are gone and continuous sweeps of cheatgrass extend for miles in all directions. Subsequent fires just perpetuate the vicious cycle and prevent the slow-growing sagebrush from ever regaining a foothold in the landscape. Because the seed source for sagebrush is also missing in these huge burns, recovery is even slower. Thus the role of fire has undergone a subversive change from a small spotty tool that maintains the shrub community to oft-repeated and widespread destructive conflagrations.

Since it is apparent that the sagebrush ecosystem is the mainstay of a number of wildlife species including the ferruginous hawk, is there any hope for curbing its demise and restoring it to sustainable wildlife habitat? As you can well imagine, the prospects of reversing such a trend are mind-boggling if not impossible. At the time I write this book, experimental efforts to recover this besieged shrub ecosystem are in their beginning stages. The Bureau of Land Management, Boise District, for example, is trying a new herbicide developed by DuPont that can be applied at one ounce per acre and effectively and selectively kill annual grasses like cheatgrass without harming established perennial bunchgrasses and shrubs. At an initial cost of roughly twenty-five dollars per acre, this chemical may hold the cheatgrass in check and allow seeded native plants a couple of years to get established.

However, no doubt several hundred million acres need recovery, and at twenty-five dollars per acre you can immediately see this will be a costly challenge. Not only will recovery cost millions of dollars a year, but it will surely take a long, long, time: probably the lifetime of your grandchildren.

Since the money to accomplish this is largely tax dollars allocated by politicians to agencies like the Bureau of Land Management, a sagebrush recovery program will be in competition for funds with live-stock grazing and other uses that prefer grassland to shrubs. Factor in burgeoning human demands such as urban sprawl and agricultural and indus-trial development on these beleaguered landscapes, and the success picture becomes increasingly bleak.

However, treasuring its touch on my life, I re-main hopeful that the shy and retiring ferruginous hawk, by the sheer grit of its versatility, will con-tinue to eke out an existence in the midst of this embattled landscape. This is my hope not just for the hawk, but also for the sake of our grandchildren. In the midst of writing this book, I experienced joy-ful initiation into grandparenthood and soon will be a grandfather for the second time. The near si-multaneous births of this book and my grandchil-dren have given rise to a new dream that I hold in my heart.

I am waiting for the day my grandchildren are old enough that I can gather them and take them on a special odyssey back to the valleys three: Curlew, Black Pine, and Raft River. I want to be able to stand where I once stood in awe, and show them ferrugi-nous hawks. I will even take them back into the Wild-cat Hills, walk with them through the pungent sagebrush and junipers to the homeland of Penelope and tell them her story. And who knows, it is quite possible that as we watch, we'll catch a glimpse of Penelope's grandchildren.

Above all, it is my hope that ferruginous hawks continue their quiet supremacy over the changing

landscape and survive the shifting political winds
so that future generations will never lack the opportunity to gaze upon and marvel at this regal hawk
in the sun.

INDEX

A

Accipiters 158, 170
adaptations 111
adaptive value 74
aerial courtship choreography 114
aeries 13
African-American 38
albino bat 113
alfalfa 156
ambient temperatures 108
ambient turbulence 114
American kestrels 117, 145, 146
Angell, Tony 169
Arco 131, 133
Arco desert 33
Armortite 126
Army-surplus metal ammunition box 19
Australian Shepherd 149, 150, 153
automobiles 129

B

badger(s) 12, 74, 165
badger burrow 112
bald eagle(s) 5, 133
baling twine 13
banding 124, 125, 126, 129
barbed wire 13
bats 114, 170
Bavarian pub 127
Bendire, Charles 13, 114
Big Sky 157
binoculars 55, 113
biologist(s) 7, 24, 106, 140, 145, 174

biotelemetry 68, 92
Bird Banding Laboratory 23
bird(s) of prey 1, 27, 62, 115, 146
black Labrador 149, 150
Black Pine 166, 180
Black Pine Valley 9, 47, 48, 138, 141
black widow spiders 87
black-billed magpie (*Pica pica*) 159
black-tailed jackrabbits 175
bleached buffalo bones 13
blind(s) 14, 17, 18, 20, 27, 28, 33, 39, 41, 43, 44, 50, 54-56, 66-69, 71, 73, 77, 81, 82, 84, 86-90, 92, 95, 97, 98-101, 105, 155, 156, 167
blowgun 136, 137
bluebirds 117
bluebonnet 30
bobcat(s) 12, 74, 85, 147, 165
body-temperature 8
Boise State University, 130
Brazilian free-tailed bats (*Tadarida braziliensis*) 170
Breeding Bird Surveys 131
broad-leaf trees 13
broad-winged hawk(s) 1, 118
Bureau of Land Management 147, 180
Bureau of Land Management, Boise District 179
butcher bird 84
buteo(s) 1, 115, 118, 158, 164, 170
Buteo regalis 5
butterflies 124

C

cache 170
caching 83, 168, 169
cactus 11
California 128
camera(s) 19-21, 27, 39, 41,
    43, 68, 72, 86, 90,
    97, 98, 127, 139
Cameron, E.S. 157, 159, 161
Canada 174
Canada lynx 173
canid 43
Canis 152
cannibalism 97
car battery 19
cardboard 13
Carlsbad Caverns National
    Park 170
carnivores 1
castings 26, 74, 145, 146
cat 160
cattle 20, 123, 145
Caucasian 38
cheatgrass (*Bromus tectorum*)
    178, 179
chicken hawks 157
chickens 157, 158
chicks 21, 26, 27, 42, 68, 79,
    81, 83, 97, 101, 109,
    111, 138, 151
Clayton, New Mexico 132
cliff-race, 115
cliffs 13
cloacal temperature 101
Coca-Cola 22, 68
Colorado 6, 145
colorful birds 76
Condor 148
cones 61
convection 110

Cooper's 119
Cooper's hawk (*A. cooperii*)
    158
cottontails 160
courtship feeding 115, 116,
    117
courtship flight 115, 117, 121
cow dung 13
coyote(s) 1-4, 12, 29, 42, 45,
    47-50, 56, 61-63, 74,
    85, 87, 128, 147, 149,
    150, 153, 164, 165, 173
Craig, Erica 133
Craig, Tim 29, 37, 44, 66,
    72-74, 76, 78, 83, 86,
    89, 90, 92, 95, 97, 131,
    133, 135-138, 144,
    146-148, 159
crepuscular 54, 106, 168, 169
crested wheat-grass. 2
Curlew 166, 180
Curlew Valley 2, 9, 72, 113,
    124, 130, 131, 153

D

deer antler 13
deer mice (*Peromyscus
    maniculatus*) 146
desert hawk 2
desert horned lizard
    (*Phrynosoma platyrhinos*)
    140, 167
desert jackrabbits 162
diet 22
displacement behavior 121
displacement/conflict
    behavior 48
dogs 149-151, 153
duck hawk 158
DuPont 179

E

eagle(s) 23, 85, 123, 145
ecologists 10, 54
ecology 49
ecotone 10
egg clutch size 15
egg-laying dates 7
electrolytes 22
Ellis, Dr. David 121
European starlings 85

F

falconer 14, 57
falconer's hood 57
falconry 136
falcons 115, 145, 158
ferruginous hawk(s) 1, 3-
    15, 18, 19, 21, 22, 25-
    28, 31, 33, 34, 36, 38,
    39, 44, 45, 47, 50, 51,
    53, 54, 56, 57, 59, 60-
    63, 65-67, 70, 74, 77,
    78, 84, 85, 87, 88, 90-
    92, 95, 96, 99, 105-
    109, 111-116, 118-121,
    123, 124, 127, 128, 130-
    133, 135, 139, 141, 144,
    149-171, 173, 174-177,
    179, 180
field mouse 160
field station 21
Five Ferrug Nest 44, 45
"flags" 13
fledging success 15
flowering plants 76
fluid 22
flutter-glide 120
flycatcher 85
follow-soar 119
food habits 15

foxes 12, 147, 165
Frank M. Chapman Fund 6
fratricide 96, 97
furry critters 76

G

Gaede, Peter 140
gape 105
gas cook stove 22
Germany 127
glucose 22
golden and bald eagles 133
golden eagle(s)
    8, 12, 62, 63, 66, 107,
    119-121, 165, 173, 175
gopher snake (Pituophis
    melanoleucus) 167
gophers 152, 153, 157
Gorp 100
Gossett, Dan 130
grant money 18
grasshopper 163
Gray's Lake 133
greasewood 10
Greasy 37, 38
Greasy ground nest 38
Great Basin 177
great horned owl(s) 54, 56,
    60-62, 89, 97, 111, 128,
    149, 162, 173
Great Plains 13, 176
Great Salt Lake Basin 9
greater sage grouse
    (Centrocercus
    urophasianus) 158
grizzly bear 173
ground nest(s) 12, 33, 37-39,
    41
ground squirrel(s) 67, 160,
    161, 175

H

habitat 7, 47, 175, 178
hallax 59
harriers 115
hatching and fledging
    success, 15
hatching dates 7
haystacks 13
heat-stress 8
Henry's Lake 133
herbicide 179
herpetological 136
herpetologists 140
hibernation 133
hicks 22
Hill Air Force Base 88
hoarding 168
horned lark (*Eremophila
    alpestris*) 159
horned lizard(s) 79, 139
horny toads 138, 139
horses 145
house sparrows 85
housecats 159
hovering 117, 118
Howard, Rich 14, 15, 21-
    23, 28, 35, 57, 59, 91,
    127, 140, 141, 143, 146,
    166, 167
human vandalism 96
hummingbirds 78
hyperthermia 107, 108
hypothermia 107

I

I.S.U. 136
Idaho 2, 6, 9, 29, 66, 102,
    124, 125, 128, 132,
    133, 161, 177

Idaho National Engineering
    Laboratory (now
    INEEL) 131, 133
Idaho State University 5, 71
Idaho-Utah border 14, 91
incubation, 44
incubation periods 7
insects 114, 142, 146
interstate highway 12
Island Park 133

J

jackrabbit(s) 10, 22, 49,
    50, 53, 60, 96, 106,
    129, 132, 133, 137, 145
    156, 160-162, 164-167,
    169, 170, 175, 176
jet bomber 88
juniper(s) 2, 9-12, 19-21,
    45, 47, 57, 58, 66, 76,
    78, 83, 85, 88, 90, 100,
    111, 113, 124, 180
Juniperus osteosperma 10

K

kangaroo rat(s) (*Dipodomys
    ordii*) 53, 67, 68, 82,
    83, 86, 87, 94, 98,
    136, 167-169, 175
kestrel 163
kingfishers 117

L

La Brea Tar Pit 140, 141
Lake Bonneville 9
leopard lizard(s) (*Gambelia
    wislizenii*) 67, 70, 137
Lewiston, Idaho 114
Linnaeus 84

Little and Big Lost River Valleys 166
livestock 29, 144, 145, 180
lizard(s) 76, 83, 99, 135, 137-140, 167, 175, 176
loggerhead shrikes 84
long-billed curlew (*Numenius americanus*) 159
Los Angeles County Museum 140

M

magpie 92
majestic hawk 5
Mario Andretti 29
meadowlark(s) 10, 41, 55, 79
medical center 60
melanistic 44, 47
Mexicali, Baja California 23
Mexico 23, 124, 128
mice 147
migration 28, 128
mini-mitter 26, 27, 67, 68, 71, 73-77, 79, 81, 92, 95, 97, 100, 101, 103, 107, 116
monarchs 124
Montana 121, 157, 159
Mormon 127
morphometrics 130
mosquitoes 87, 95
mountain quail 99
mourning doves 90
mouse 163
movie cameras 18
mule deer 123

N

Nampa, Idaho 107
natal nest tree 130
naturalist(s) 42, 135, 139, 145, 153
Negro 38
nest(s) 7, 8, 11-14, 17-19, 21, 26-28, 30, 31, 34-36, 38, 42-45, 47-49, 51, 54, 55, 57, 58, 60, 66, 70, 72-74, 78, 79, 81, 83, 84, 86, 92, 95, 96, 98, 101, 102, 105, 109-112, 116, 138, 149-152, 155-158, 166, 176
nestling(s) 23, 50, 53, 54, 58, 60, 61, 70, 74, 78, 81-83, 86, 92-94, 96, 98, 103, 105, 106, 109, 110, 117, 124, 128, 130, 164
New Mexico 128
nocturnal vision. 61
North America 25, 67, 177
North Dakota 128
northern goshawk (*Accipiter gentilis*) 158
northern harrier(s) 54, 115, 120, 141
northern shrike (*Lanius excubitor*) 84
"numbers game" 77

O

Odysseus 28
Old Barn 157, 161
Old Barn Nest 156, 168
ornithologist 114
out-buildings 13
owls 144

P

packrats 74
painted ladies 124
parasites 74
parasol 109
parasolled, 70
patagium 126
pellets 145
Penelope 28, 30, 31, 33,
    34, 60, 66-68, 70-73,
    75-79, 81-84, 86, 92,
    95-99, 102, 105, 110,
    137, 180
peregrine falcon (*Falco
    perigrinus*) 5, 158
perennial bunchgrass(es)
    177, 178
phlox 30
photographs 26
photosynthetic molecules
    171
Physiology 106
Planet Earth 114
plastic 13
Pocatello 57, 60, 71, 95
pocket gopher(s) 151, 156,
    160, 161, 168
prairie 13
prairie dog(s) 160, 161, 171
prairie falcon 145
predation 45, 50, 60, 85,
    128, 163
predator(s) 1, 49, 51, 58,
    62, 77, 83, 96, 125, 139,
    144, 147, 157, 160-162,
    165
predatory 96
Protestant 127
psychologists 120
pygmy rabbits 177

R

rabbit(s) 133, 160, 162,
    163, 165, 166, 169,
    171
radio transmitters 26
Raft River 180
Raft River Valley 9, 44, 166
raptor(s) 5, 7, 8, 12, 29, 53,
    54, 68, 74, 84, 96, 114,
    116, 117, 119, 120, 126,
    130, 143-147, 158,
    165, 169, 175
raptor biologist(s) 6, 13
raptor biology 7
raptor flight control tower
    54
raptor species 107
rattlesnakes
    79, 86, 87, 89, 139
raven(s) 123, 141-143
red-tailed hawk 11, 54, 115,
    170
regal or majestic hawk 5
rehabilitation 21
research budget 18, 33
Richardson's ground squir-
    rels 133
ring-necked pheasants
    (*Phasianus colchicus*) 159
"rings of bones" 13
robin 56
rock wrens 90
Rocky Mountains 133
rodent(s) 160, 161, 167, 169
rods 61
rough-legged hawk 118-
    120, 164
Russian thistles 124

S

Saflag 126
sage 54, 155
sage grouse 173, 176, 177
sage sparrows 176
sage thrashers 176, 177
sagebrush 2, 9, 10, 11, 13,
    22, 34, 35, 41, 62, 75,
    113, 124, 164, 169,
    170, 177, 179, 180
sagebrush ecosystem
    178, 179
sagebrush lizard 176
sagebrush-perenial grass
    ecosystem(s) 175, 176
Salt Lake basin 87
scavengers 125, 143, 147
scorpions 87
sharp-shinned hawk (*A.
    striatus*) 119, 158
sharp-tailed grouse
    (*Tympanuchus
    phasianellus*) 158, 159
sheep 123, 145
short-eared owl(s) 54-56,
    119, 136, 149
shot 129
shrub-grass landscape 30
shrub-steppe 176, 177
size differences 15
sky-dance 115
Snake River canyon 66
snakes 76, 87, 137, 140
snow squall 30
snowshoe hares 162
Snowville 30, 37, 156
Snowville Café 136
Snowville, Utah 27
snowy owls 48
songbird 67

Southwest 124
Spanish 23
spotted owl 5
spotting scope 2, 18, 30,
    35, 38, 41, 42, 47, 67,
    79, 93, 151
Squirrel Hawk 160
stampede 123, 124
State of Washington 174
Stone, Idaho, 130
Strongfield, Saskatchewan,
    Canada. 132
Swainson's hawk(s) 11,
    54, 119, 120, 138

T

talons 11, 59, 60, 84, 115,
    155, 164, 165
tape recorder 42
tar pit 129
telethermometer 69, 97, 101
terra firma 164
tetanus 60
tetanus-causing pathogens
    60
Texas 128
thermoregulate 99
thermoregulatory 8, 15
thermoregulatory
    behavior(s) 26, 102, 110
time-lapse camera 20
time-lapse photography 14
titmouse 90
tomial tooth 84
translator 23
Trost, Dr. Chuck 8, 15, 66,
    68, 71, 127
tularemia 60
tumbleweeds 123

U

U.S. Fish and Wildlife
    Service 173
UFO 88
United States
    8, 115, 124, 174
Utah 6, 9, 12, 27, 29, 109,
    128, 136
Utah juniper 10
utility poles 13

V

V-W squareback 29, 56, 76,
    136
valley pocket gopher,
    (*Thomomys townsendii*)
    161
vascularized 106
veterinarian 57, 60
vole(s) 156, 160

W

Washington State 109, 169
West 85, 125, 147, 162,
    177, 178
western kingbirds 85
western meadowlark
    (*Sternella neglecta*) 159
western whiptail
    (*Cnemidophorus tigris*)
    137, 167
Westerners 177
white butterfly 113
white-tailed jackrabbit
    (*Lepus townsendii*) 161
Wildcat Hills 27-29, 34, 37,
    44, 67, 86-88, 95, 124,
    137, 180
Wilson, Edward O. 91

windmills 13
woodrat 74
wormwood 178

Z

Zane Grey 123
zygodactylous 60

ORDER FORM

Name _____

Address _____

City/State/Zip _____

Phone _____

Enclosed is my check or credit card for $18.45 ($14.95 for A HAWK IN THE SUN and $3.50 for shipping and handling.)

Credit card _____

(VISA or MC accepted)

Expiration date _____

DIMI PRESS
3820 Oak Hollow Lane, SE
Salem, OR 97302-4774

Call toll-free: 800-644-DIMI(3464) for orders
Phone 503-364-7698 for information
FAX 503-364-9727
E-mail: dickbook@earthlink.net
Web: http://home.earthlink.net/~dickbook